SEPARATING FROM THE PACK

DORIAN JONES

PREFACE

Where I come from, we aren't worried about building the future; we are more focused on day-to-day survival. I was never taught the value of personal growth, let alone knew it was an actual thing. Over the years, I grew as an individual and began to learn valuable life lessons. These lessons allowed me to grow in a different direction than the norm in my community. I developed many skills over my teenage and adult years that would later help me grow into the well-rounded man I am today. I never tried to use excuses or look for people to give me a handout because of my circumstances. All I ever wanted was an opportunity, which I decided to create for myself. This book is just a segway into what I have planned. I wrote this book so that those who feel stuck will have a help guide to get on the right track to take control of their life.

I want all people that feel lost or uncertain about life, those who aren't happy or just want to make a shift from the norm, to find encouragement in this book. There are so many examples on display every day that show that you can come from any circumstance and make amazing things happen. This is me reaching my hand back; to help you Separate From The Pack.

Don't be scared, hold my hand tight! Breakaway with all of your strength! When you feel any force pulling you back, you pull even harder and fight for your destiny. Remember, EVERYBODY HAS GREATNESS WITHIN, EVEN YOU!

Dorian Jones

SEPARATING FROM THE PACK

TABLE OF CONTENTS

INTRO

I f you're reading this, I guess that you are seeking to live a better life. Just trying to figure it all out so that you can create an extraordinary experience, but you got lost or slowed up somewhere along the way. You had this vision of being this person you created in your mind that lived a life very different from what you were used to, but it just didn't happen quite as planned. You may feel stuck and asking yourself, "How can I change this?" or "What's next?"

You may feel like your days just go by, and everything is repetitive. You wake up, go to work, come home tired, eat, sleep, and repeat. Or you've been working at a job that just seems like it isn't going anywhere or realizing that it's not what you want anymore. You could even be depressed, which is dangerous, especially if you don't know it. I want to tell you that you are not alone. When we attempt to make progress, there will always be something or someone to slow us down; this could be either internal or external sources. This resistance is so strong that many may stop trying to fight it and remain stagnant. Did you know that a high percentage of adults are currently unhappy? There are way too many who are not satisfied with how their lives have turned out and feel stuck. To put it in the purest form, the best way to get over this is to shift your mindset, take action, and continue moving. I know that it is easier said than done. So I wrote this book to assist you with the transition needed to reconstruct your life and *Separate From The Pack*. If you don't know what I'm talking about, I'm talking about the pack of settling for average.

No matter where you are from or where you grew up, I'm sure you can identify the average of your life. If you can't, let me briefly explain. What I am referring to is the expectations that people have for you based on your upbringing. What did the average adult around you have or do? That is the pack that I am referencing. But you, you want to get beyond average, and I get it, consider this my helping hand to help pull you away from the pack. Pulling away from the pack of mediocrity, poverty, self-doubt, or whatever else is potentially holding you back.

Before we go any further, I'd like you to understand what this book is and isn't. This is not:

- A how-to get wealthy or successful book.
- A book to solve your problems for you.
- A financial guide book(there are some references).
- An autobiography about my life.
- For everyone

This is:

- A "How can I separate and blaze my own path" book.
- A guide to help you get on the right track.
- A guideline to help shift your thinking to get the results that you desire.
- A book for the average person that's trying to live a life by design and not by default.
- For those who are not happy with where they are and don't know precisely how to change their situation.

To get the best results from this material, you must take action. There are certain things I may repeat a few times throughout the book just to make sure it drives home the point. Certain principles are essential for growth in every part of your life. They include mindset, setting goals, taking action, and persisting, just to name a few.

I have a real passion for success, whether that be my success or someone else's. I simply love seeing people win; I get excited seeing an underdog come out on top. It is no secret that life isn't an even playing field for all. I believe that there is no excuse for why you can't go out and become great in your own right. Some may have a head start in the race and a clear path, but those that start late or have obstacles can come out on top as well. It can be discouraging when you see others achieving things that you feel you should have done already.

There is no need for you to feel discouraged, especially if you are still working on yourself and your goals. Everyone is on their clock and will get what's meant for them when intended for them to get it. Until that time comes, you must believe and keep doing the work to accumulate into the results you desire. I have been presented with many obstacles throughout my life. Some of which I felt like I would never make it through. I am a living testament that you will overcome anything if you believe and have a clear vision for your future. As I was going through my hard times, I felt no end to my struggles. I continued to push forward because I knew that it couldn't last forever. Along the path, my thinking changed, and the results changed right along with it. I became more careful with my actions and choice of words towards myself and others, realizing that what I said and truly believed is what becomes my reality.

This book was always just an idea. I had this idea of writing a book someday, but about what? I'd flirt around with these different ideas, never really being serious about any of them. I eventually discovered my purpose and passion for helping others become better. That is one of the factors that led to this book. I feel that I have experienced enough in life to assist others who may have to deal with some of the obstacles that I've overcome in life. Now be honest, do you believe that you can achieve anything in this world? When I say anything, I mean it. Do you think you can change the world, assume massive wealth, or just be the man or woman calling the shots in your life? Or whatever it is that you can imagine. Some people think it is just a dream and not possible, but I am here to tell you that you can become whatever you want with the proper mindset, preparation, and action. Of course, you can always talk about what you want to do and how you'll do it, but doing it is a different story. Having the courage and guts to commit and go after something that isn't the norm is a significant risk. It's not a risk if you are willing to do whatever you have to do to live the life of your dreams. The real danger is never trying to do anything and living with regrets asking yourself, what if? Remember, it is only fantasy if you don't believe you can have it. If you can dream it, you can achieve it, but only when you pair your plans with sincere belief and action. It becomes easy to do when you have the right tools in your toolbox as well.

One of the main tools, which is my favorite is the mindset. I discovered the power of mindset in my journey. As a young adult, I had a rough time being depressed and feeling sorry for myself. Until one day, I had a wake-up call and decided that I would take control of my life from there on out. That was the best decision I had ever made. That one decision opened so many doors for me and allowed me to cultivate relationships that wouldn't have been possible if I had not made that decision. If I hadn't made the shift, I'd be stuck in the same cycle and have those same feelings come over me more frequently.

I whole-heartedly hope you learn something from this material. It is a mixture of practical steps, my true beliefs, and the foundation for achieving your wildest dreams. This book is for the everyday man and woman that live an ordinary life within the pack but now want to separate and live a life that they designed. All of these things included here are coming from my observations, experience, trials, and tribulations. You will get maximum results from the book if you are honest with yourself, know where you currently stand, and are serious about experiencing a change. We always ask for things but don't take the necessary steps to make the changes we want. That must stop here; no more excuses, procrastination, or being lazy. Get ready to get off your ass and get uncomfortable. Yes, it comes with change. When we disrupt our observed behavior, we will naturally resist. I want you to be aware of the resistance as it happens and be ready to fight it. I understood this once I started waking up early. I'd wake up, lay in bed, get on my phone, and do everything except get out of the bed. Once I pushed myself to just get out of the bed, the rest became easy. After a week of doing it, it was natural. Don't make the mistake of confusing your resistance with anything other than growth.

My Discovery

My journey began one late night while I was brainstorming. I couldn't sleep this particular night, tossing and turning, and no matter how I positioned myself, I couldn't sleep. I thought to myself, "Why are some people more successful than others? Why are some people happier than others?" This set me on an inquisitive journey. As far as I can recall, I had always been inquisitive. I would dig deeper into things that caught my interest and learned as much as I possibly could on the subject. I had huge goals that I wanted to achieve and didn't know how to get there, so I began reading and studying anything I can get my hands on that talked about goal achievement. I would read the profiles of people who have achieved great things in life, and

I realized that people put their mistakes out there for us to learn from them so that we can have an easier time accomplishing our goals. Like one of my idols, Jay-Z said, "Hov did that, so hopefully, you won't have to go through that." In my discovery, it became evident that success and happiness are not accidental or inborn. I had seen enough proof for the answer to be apparent that happiness and success were achieved internally and overtime. During this time, I realized that happiness or success aren't things you can buy. If you believe that money can buy happiness, you are mistaken.

The achievement of success is a roller coaster with highs and lows, twists and turns, and surprises, and on this ride, you learn your true self. If you want something bad enough, you'll find a way to enjoy the ride. The images of success that are commonly portrayed are false. Mainstream media creates this glamorous, flawless lifestyle around success. The road to success itself is a dirty, muddy, pothole-filled road. It does get smoother the longer you're on it, but it never really gets easy. It is a constant uphill climb. Just as if you were working out, the more you run on the incline, the easier it becomes., but the burn is still there.

After coming to this conclusion, it was only right for me to dig even deeper, I eventually stumbled upon the subject of personal development. Personal development is a broad subject and has many sub-categories underneath it. In my initial research stages, I had come across the works of people like Eric Thomas, Grant Cardone, Brendon Burchard, Tony Robbins, Les Brown, and Brian Tracy, just to name a few. Every time I discovered these individuals, I'd dig deeper into their work and career.

After years of being fascinated by this subject, I decided to jump in and take action myself. This step unlocked a new passion for me. That passion turned out to be the mindset. Never would I have imagined myself writing an actual book because of this discovery. While there are already numerous books on this subject, I'm more than certain that I have a unique perspective on the subject. Being a young black male who grew up on government assistance in a low-income housing development in Los Angeles, I have a different perspective on my discovery of the subject.

Your mindset is a compilation of different experiences and beliefs, the good and the bad you experience in life all contribute to your mindset. Some are conscious of it, but many are not. The moment you sit back and think about ways to improve your life, you are now ready to take control of your mindset. You are becoming aware of a part of your brain that we don't put to regular use, the subconscious mind. The subconscious mind is one that you must learn to access and control. Knowing this and taking control of your thinking is a skill in itself. It takes a lot of self-discovery and deep reflection to understand your thoughts. Everyone has voices in their head, and these voices can act as a motivator or be the complete opposite. These voices in our heads are trained by things we see and the thoughts that we think the most. So if you are always thinking about something terrible or focus more on the negatives, that voice will gladly serve you negativity in return. The choice is yours, whether that voice feeds on positives or negatives. Shifting our mindset will help guide our minds in the right direction.

When in deep thought, I sometimes think about the place I grew up. I analyzed things that happened in my life, people I grew up around and realized that the idea of "mindset" was never presented to us. I know for a fact that I had never thought about my mindset in my previous years. "Mindset? What the f*** is that?" is something the younger me would say. I felt that it wasn't fair that you have millions, maybe even billions of people who were uneducated as well. How can you expect someone to learn something if it isn't taught? Many of us will never take our education beyond the schooling that we receive.

Aside from homework, more research was the last thing on our minds. I began to brainstorm a way that I can share my discovery and this new passion for developing a growth mindset. It came to me right away; why not share the message in the same way that these other people I studied did. I'll express my knowledge via the internet, literature, and other means I can employ to get the message out to the world. I had so many doubts and fears in this process. I think we have all had those "what if" moments. You know the ones where you think of all of the worst things that can happen and allow them to stop you from taking action. I would always think of what could go wrong, not what can go right. I'd talk myself out of it before taking any action on it. I also accepted that I don't know everything on the subject, and many people may challenge my pattern of thoughts. I am okay with that, and I am confident in anything that I put out and have enough knowledge to back it up. I never claim to know everything; there is always an opportunity for growth in my life. Everything that I'm saying may not work for every single individual in the world. I encourage you to research things yourself. These are some of the things that helped shape my life and put me on the path to achieving anything that I put into my mind.

Get Out Of Your Head

It all starts in your mind. I discovered that happy people do not give up on their dreams or things they believe in. When the road gets rough, they are buckling up and enjoying the ride. I am talking about the dreamers, hustlers, and go-getters who keep going no matter what. Then there are other sets of people - some who let roadblocks stop them in their tracks, and they get stuck, or the people who are content with their situations and find comfort in their lifestyle. If you set out to get more and stop, this is considered settling; it will eventually lead to unhappiness. This unhappiness can linger on for years or a lifetime. I feel it is unfair to some because they don't know any better and have no clue what to do to stop this. Everyone should set some type of goal for themselves and go after it no matter what. No one should be looked down on because of their status or shoot themselves down because they've never attempted to change their situation. Life is tough, everyone has their own set of problems, but we all have the same opportunities. We don't always realize the opportunities in our faces because we are too busy looking at the problem and what others have. Most people we consider "successful" never worry about the next person's journey; they are too busy focusing on their own.

In my mind, I figured that there must be something these successful individuals possess that those who quit, give up, fail, or never get started didn't have. I discovered there are three different types of people. The first is uneducated on the basics of adulthood. These individuals are programmed from a young age to believe they are limited to things based on the circumstances and resources they are given. The second type is taught that there are no limits to what they can achieve in life. They feel entitled to the things that they were told they should or could have. Finally, you have individuals who come from the first group but educate themselves and discover that there are no limits on life besides the ones we put on ourselves, and they get in the driver's seat of their life. I was raised in an environment where most people are a product of their surroundings, but I wanted better. I learned valuable lessons over my teenage years and young adult life. Through all of my experiences, I became more wise and always sought to gain more knowledge. I intentionally sought out growth opportunities.

Allow me the opportunity to educate, and enlighten you on the potential you have within and to help you realize it. This book shall be a guide to help you achieve any goal that you can imagine and find happiness in any part of your life. I will cover principles that, if lived by, will help you Separate From The Pack, maximize the results in your life, and help you become the best version of yourself. If you apply these things, you will live a more fulfilling life and unlock new ideas that have been deep inside you this whole time. These are meant to be practical and actionable steps that, if put to daily use, will bring you happiness and success in every part of your life that you desire. You will realize you can conquer the world, and nobody can stop you. It is meant to give you that mental energy that so many people lack. That sense of drive that we may sometimes lose just by going through life. If I can help 1% of the world's population, I will achieve my goal.

Personal development is very interesting. It is a continuous process that will happen throughout life. You will be on a never-ending rollercoaster. You'll have lows as deep as the ocean depths and highs as high as Mt. Everest. This journey is exciting because it will mold you into that unique YOU. It can change you for the better or worse. Your willingness and capacity to handle all challenges and obstacles thrown at you will determine your growth. Nobody comes up saying that they want to be unhappy or just want to get halfway up the ladder and be satisfied. It is so easy to get sucked into life's sinkholes, lose hope, and take the energy-sucking jabs that are thrown at you day in and day out. That's no way to live at all. I love this whole concept of people's life journey because everyone is unique, and no matter where you are from, you should achieve YOUR happiness. Everyone has or had a dream. If you have an idea, you've picked the right book. If you have a dream, you've chosen the right book. I wholeheartedly believe that achieving any goal is as simple as envisioning, planning, persisting, and executing. There are a lot of small steps between these things that you must encounter.

Personal development is essential to human growth. It is a compilation of learning and growing from your ups and downs, trials and tribulations, defeat and triumph. It is a lifelong learning experience that comes in many forms, and it has no favorites. I love to see people go through tough things and still come out on top, which is no easy venture. Coming out of tough situations requires a lot of strong will and drive. You have to be willing to stick through it, and your desire to change must be ten times stronger than the pain you are feeling. This mindset develops over time; it is not inborn. Everyone has faced some sort of challenge in their life and has gotten through it and felt better about themselves because of it. Not everyone can say that they were able to move on. They may not possess the drive or energy to push through. Sometimes we need guidance and someone to hold our hand to guide us in the dark so that we can catch our balance. This hand isn't always there, there were times when I needed that hand, and it was nowhere to be found, but I figured it out. Getting over those tough times was one of my inspirations for getting into personal development and helping others who need that helping hand. This book is my helping hand to anyone who may feel themselves slipping or perhaps need an extra push to go to the next level.

This book is written with you in mind, the person that is eager to make a change but needs a little guidance. After reading this book, you should feel that you can overcome all obstacles that come your way. You should also develop a clear vision of an outlook of your future. This book will teach you how to become a better person to achieve great things in life. We are already equipped with everything we need to achieve anything we can imagine. I'd like to ask you to open your mind while reading this book and allow your mind to become a sponge to it all.

MY MINDSET SHIFT:
"How I Got My Mind Right"

A mindset shift occurs when you have an "ah-ha moment." Things suddenly make sense to you, and you see life from a much wider perspective. You begin to make different choices than the ones you would have previously made. I remember the time when my first real mindset shift occurred. It came in the spring/summer of 2017 when I first got serious about learning more about Real Estate Investing; I had picked up a book by Robert Kiyosaki titled "Cashflow Quadrant." This book is a part of the Rich Dad Poor Dad series. Many people would read Rich Dad Poor Dad(which I did eventually read later) before this book. The thing that caught my attention was the Cashflow Quadrant. Let me explain the quadrant itself to create a better understanding. You have a square with each corner representing a quadrant:

At the top left corner, you have the "E" Employee Quadrant.

At the bottom left, you have the "S" Self-Employed Quadrant.

At the top right corner, you have the "B" Business owner Quadrant.

Finally, at the bottom right, you have the "I" Investor quadrant.

- People in the" E" quadrant earn their income from a job.
- People in the "S" quadrant work for themselves, maybe freelancers or contract workers whose income is based on the job they perform or contracts they receive.
- People in the "B" quadrant own a business or multiple, such as franchises or any other type of business system.
- People in the "I" quadrant are people who put their money to work, meaning they'll invest and get paid off of returns or profits from their investment.

This chart was fascinating to me. It was right up my alley; at the time, I was in the "E" quadrant wanting to jump to the right side of the quadrant. As I read this book, I realized that there is so much that I didn't know, so much simple information, yet it was foreign to me. I feel like I was given the wrong information up until this point in my life. Now I had solid knowledge to redo my life's blueprint that I was using to build the foundation of my future. Even though I had been running my clothing brand and had taught myself everything I knew with the help of reading, trial and error, YouTube, and Google. There was still so much knowledge that I lacked.

Just being an observer of the world got me thinking about all of the endless possibilities that a small percentage of us take advantage of. Everything is out there for us to get. I then thought back on my upbringing and environment and asked myself what influences and positive role models I had access to. There weren't many if any, at all. I wanted to change that as an individual; I wanted to become a role model that the people can relate with. I set out on a mission to change the narrative of the black male from my community. It is very important for me to show the kids coming from similar backgrounds as mine the importance of educating themselves and other ways out. You can stand out and still be a part of your community; you shouldn't feel like you don't belong somewhere because of your choice to do something that isn't the norm. In most black communities, the only people outside of the hood that we know to look up to are entertainers, whether a rapper, a singer, an actor or an athlete. We look at these means as our only way out. The majority of us dream of being a star athlete or superstar rap artist. I wanted to change that narrative. I want to show everyone that you can be different and make it while remaining true to your roots and not forgetting your roots. This whole thought process made me think bigger and set audacious goals for myself. How can I go bigger? This is something I often ask myself, even to this day. How can little ole me make a big ole impact?

Early Life Inspirations

Seeing the things I saw as a kid was a lot, from murders to drug dealing and general gang activity. It shouldn't have been normal to hear gunshots or know to run when a car comes speeding down the street, but it was my normal experience. I loved my childhood, and I had fun, from playing sports in the streets, slap boxing, bean shooters, and getting wet with the water hose and anything else we could get into; I wouldn't change a thing. As I got older, my interest changed, and my mind developed a bit more. I got more serious about basketball and would usually play year-round, so I'll travel to different city locations to play other teams. While these locations weren't that far away, they were foreign to me, and on the rides there, I'd see things that I hadn't seen before. I was fascinated by the smallest of things that were so close but seemed so far. It opened up my mind and made me want to explore more outside my neighborhood. Once I reached 14 or 15 years of age, I would have my mom drop me off at the Green Line station, and I would ride the train and go to the Lakewood Mall or Manhattan Beach. Going to these locations provided extraordinary experiences for me. I was able to see how people lived and functioned outside of Watts. The Lakewood Mall was a Los Angeles suburb that is close to Long Beach, so other teenagers were also hanging out here on the weekends from schools out that way. We didn't have any safe hang-out spots in my neighborhood besides the park, and at any given moment, it could become a warzone. Manhattan Beach is a little south of LAX and is a small beach community. I used to go to Fry's Electronics on Rosecrans and Sepulveda to buy pieces to put onto the PC that I had at home. I'd find any excuse to get out of my hood.

The real exploration came when I was about 19 years old, and I began to drive. I'd drive up to Beverly Hills and Hollywood, and I was fascinated. This is all new to me, and I'd drive up the hills and be mesmerized by the homes hanging off the hill with a view of the city or ocean. Or I'd just people watch, and it was all new and fascinating to me. This was a very critical part of my early adult life. I discovered a Beverly Hills car dealership on Olympic just one block west of Robertson Blvd. Not just any dealership, this location sold Spyker, Bentley, Lamborghini, Aston Martin, Bugatti, and Rolls Royce at the time. Until then, I had only seen these cars on the internet and fantasized about them. I decided to pay this dealership a visit and window shop; touching these cars gave me this jolt of energy that I can not explain until this day. I'd meet a lot of their actual clients coming in to buy cars or get theirs serviced. I'd just converse with them; no real conversations, just small talk. More than anything, they were shocked to see a young black male in a place like that. I'd dress like a "Hip-Hop" artist(you know the stereotype), so I assume that they thought I was in the music business(just my assumption). Eventually, one of the guys got used to seeing me there and took me on a test drive in the newly released Bentley Continental GT. It was gloss black with black rims, red brake calipers, and a black interior with red stitching. On this drive, he talked to me. He asked me questions about my personal life and what I did. I told him that I loved the cars and would eventually own a few of them one day. He looked me in the eyes, smiled, and said, "One day, you will have these cars just because you believe you can have them, but you have to work hard for it." He knew I couldn't afford it at the time but admired my ambition. What he did next changed my life forever. He pulled over and told me to get behind the wheel. "For real?! Me? Drive this? Are you sure?" He shook his head as we both exited the car. I was pretty sure that he shouldn't let me behind the wheel. My heart was racing, and my palms were sweating. I was really behind this machine that I had only dreamed of. This was a different feeling than my green 1998 Oldsmobile Cutlass Supreme(which I kept clean). The feel of the leather on the steering wheel and seeing that "B" sit between the wings staring me right in the face as I prepared to accelerate still felt like a dream. I was on a street that had a straight way, and then he told me to floor it. So I did just that, I put my foot to the gas and went from 0-60MPH in about 3-4 seconds. The torque pinned me down to the seat as I sped down this empty residential street in Beverly Hills. Ever since that moment, my life has never been the same. That moment and conversation taught me a great lesson. If you can dream it, you can achieve it, and if you can touch it, you can have it. Some will call it a tease, but for me, it was motivation.

Your Mindset Shift

Enough about me, let's talk about you. What is your current mindset? Are you uncertain, confused, focused, or just lost in space? The first step to shifting your mind is knowing your current mindset and where you'd like to guide it. How do you expect to go somewhere if you don't know where you are coming from? Once you have identified your current mindset, you can now focus on your next action step to move on to the next level. There is no right or wrong mindset; everyone has had to deal with them at one point or the other, sometimes you deal with multiple concurrently. Awareness is the key when it comes to shifting your thinking. Identifying where you are right now is the most important thing you can do for your personal growth. It is so easy to get caught up in life; things move so fast, you see people living the picture-perfect life, ads telling you what you need to have or do to be beautiful or successful. Life can get overwhelming and full of bullshit, especially with so much going on, excluding the day-to-day grind. I know that it gets hard, but you must find the small crack in those dark clouds. Trust me; it's there; just keep searching, and it'll appear. I am speaking from experience; I've been through depression, questioning my existence on earth, and using the last of my energy to not fall into a life of crime. So trust me when I tell you that IT WILL GET BETTER! It takes time, dedication, and patience. In this time, you must learn from the experiences that you are being presented with and allow them to create a stronger you. Learn to analyze things going on in your life to find the gem in the mess that you are being dealt with.

Have you gotten through dark clouds, or have they stopped you? Be honest with yourself. Once you are honest with yourself, it becomes much easier to find the path that will help you elevate to the next phase, now you are ready to unleash your greatness and become a better and newer version of yourself. Your future is all dependent on you and only you. You must think about it, visualize it, and speak it into existence. Remember to commit and take the actions necessary for you to get closer to that goal. As long as you are moving towards something, it will return the favor and meet you halfway. Once this thinking becomes a part of your conscious mind, you will be unstoppable.

REALLY THOUGH! WHAT IS SUCCESS?

How do you define success? Whatever your answer is, how did you come up with that answer, and why is that your answer? What is it about this thing that makes it mean success to you? I know that these questions will challenge some, and that's okay. For me, being successful means making an impact bigger than me; I mean way bigger than me. I've always thought on a large scale, and I'm talking about the type of stuff that can have people thinking I am crazy. Success is being able to make an impact on people's lives, to help others be happy and achieve their wildest dreams, along with doing the things that bring me joy on my terms. I truly get a thrill from seeing others living up to their fullest potential or at least pushing towards it, whatever that may be. As stated earlier in this book, I noticed that personal development was a passion of mine, and it is something that I enjoy all facets of. From being the underdog to the come-up, it's nice watching it all unfold. Remember that you must first be successful as a person before you are successful in anything else. To me, being successful as a person means(but is not limited to) being kind to others and finding your happiness in life. Whatever you do, always have your best interest in mind; you must have your own back. Despite having a family, a job, or whatever other obligations you have, you must find the time to focus on your well-being and discover your happiness. How can you possibly give your best towards something else if you aren't happy within?

I've always known that I wanted to achieve a lot in life. I set huge goals for myself. I am determined to show the world that I came from nothing and made it happen for myself; with no handouts, I did the hard work, made the sacrifices, put myself in position, and built relationships, truly self-made. It's alright to be different, just DO YOU. Growing up in a poverty-stricken, gang, and drug-infested environment, you can feel trapped or like your options are limited. You may have heard of the crabs in a barrel mentality, well it is real. The moment they see someone climbing out, they are pulled right back down into the bucket. I saw beyond that and knew that there was more to life, and I had to escape that barrel. I knew that there were better parts of the world that I had not seen. I knew to escape that Barrell, I had to overcome the mental trap that I was in. I had to seek out information that wasn't present in my immediate circumstances. I made a vow to myself that I would escape this cycle and become the person I know I can be.

Some people define success by how much money they have, what title they hold, the car they drive, or the house they live in. While these things do fuel your ego and are great ways to reward yourself, they don't define success. Success is something that money can't buy. It is something that can't be taken away from you. It goes beyond a feeling or an emotion; it is a mission. You can work a minimum wage job and feel successful, as long as you can sleep at the end of the day with a smile on your face knowing you are contributing to making the world a better place. Many people have money and material things but remain unhappy, while others have the bare minimum and smile every day. Seeing these "successful" images portrayed in public can make some feel insecure or like a failure. Remember that you define your success. To the people who may have those thoughts, I say this; everyone is on their personal clock, focus on your personal growth, and good things will come to you when the time is right. Learn to use others' success as fuel for your fire and drive; never compare yourself or get discouraged. Seeing someone else that has reached their success should be a testament that you can do it too. We all have the same 24 hours and breathe the same air. All the necessary resources will come to you at the right time as long as you are investing in yourself and doing the internal work to elevate your mind and make the moves to get to the next level. As I said before, if you move towards something, that same thing will meet you halfway.

Success Is...Or Isn't...

We have been fed with this imagery of successful people being rich from an early age. Holding high positions, having big houses, and driving expensive cars. While those things are all nice, they mean nothing if the people who are fortunate enough to have acquired them have poor morals or if they are unhappy. We've all come across such people; they have bad attitudes, they think they are better because of their position, or look down on others who can't help them or that don't "look the part." These individuals are insecure, and their current possessions are a blanket that makes them feel like they have power. These types of people don't last very long. Rich or poor, it is your choice to decide how you'll treat others. The little guy won't always be the little guy. You never know who will morph into someone you may need later in life. Learn not to base your success on physical possessions. Instead, base them on things that money can't buy. What will you do to make your legacy live on long after you're gone?

Success is that feeling of fulfillment, that sense of pride that you carry with you. That feeling comes in different forms for everybody. Some of us get the feeling when we can change someone else's life, while others get it when they accomplish a difficult task. Success comes to you all of your life. You will have many moments of success. You are successful every day if you can walk away with a smile on your face and feeling good about yourself. Whether that joy comes from an act you did for someone else or something you accomplished for yourself, the feeling of success and accomplishment can come every day if you look for it. Don't ever let anyone or anything steal your pride and happiness. You worked hard to feel this way, and you should wear your success proudly. You should never feel that you should hold back your happiness to make someone else comfortable and you should stop hanging around people that make you feel that way.

How Can You Attain YOUR Success

Attaining success may never come across some people's minds. Many just live life one day at a time and never think about finding true happiness. We are sucked into the wormhole of life and have everything sucked out of us. Life then gets repetitive, and you are now a robot. You wake up, do your same morning routine, same traffic, same job duties, same frustrations day in and day out. A very high percentage of us deal with this for most, if not all, of our adult lives. It's not your fault; most of us are programmed this way, but it is your fault if you are unhappy and don't take steps to change it. As humans, we are scared to take risks, especially risks with no guarantee that they'll work out as planned. We feel most comfortable in our comfort zone where we are sure of results. Taking risks has no safety net; you will have to grow your wings and build your safety net the moment you jump off the cliff. If you never take a leap of faith, you will live a life of regret. With a job, you know that you'll retire and have been able to save some percentage of your money, pension, or whatever other savings you can acquire from the blood-sucking job. While engaging in your day-to-day duties, you've forgotten about yourself, your dreams, and your happiness.

You've stopped working on yourself, and you've given in to the overwhelming tasks of everyday life. If this sounds familiar, good. This is a wake-up call; it's time to take control of your life and become the navigator. This is a new age where you choose your destiny, and no one can determine your worth.

To effect this change, some things need to take place. Developing certain habits is what is going to get you out of that cycle. Practices such as focus, commitment, staying healthy, persistence, and being passionate, are just a few. I'll break each of them down for you, explaining why they are essential and how you can start applying them today.

- Focus allows you to stay on course with something. You are not easily distracted. You can regain momentum with little or no effort.

- Commitment to something takes dedication and sacrifice. Once you commit to something, you must be fully engaged in whatever it is that you've committed to and see it all the way through.

- Have you ever heard the saying, "your health is your wealth"? How do you expect to do something if you aren't physically, mentally, or emotionally fit? Yes, your health is more than just exercising. You must learn to balance all aspects of your health. Mental, emotional, physical, social, and spiritual.

- The greatest achievers are all persistent in their efforts. You can't start and go on to the next thing while leaving something unfinished. No matter how hard things may be at any given time, you must not give up.

- You need to be passionate, a burning desire to be and do better. You feel this in your heart; it is something you must do for yourself. Without passion, it is easy for you to quit something without a fight once things become tough (and they will).

If you are applying these principles to your daily life, the results will be astounding. You'll get more done, feel different, more confident, and have more sense of purpose. Before you know it, seemingly big things will become very easy for you. You'll learn to break them up into pieces and bring them all together once the time is right. It's amazing what you can do with just a little change in your routine. Take control of your future, visualize your future, and put a plan in place to help you get closer to your goals and ideal life. These little things are overlooked continuously by many because of the lack of visible immediate results. Those small triumphs are meant to be a segway to the big results that you are looking for. You can't reach home plate without touching 1st, 2nd, and 3rd base first. You'll never get to the top of a mountain by only taking one step.

WHY DO SOME PEOPLE ACHIEVE MORE?

To answer this question in simple terms, "some people work harder than others." However, the answer is more complicated than that. As kids and teenagers, we all had our "dream" job and this "dream" life that we pictured. We were in a specific career, married to this fantasy person, and whatever else your imagination could birth. This is how our life would turn out in our minds because we were told anything is possible, just believe. What happens to these dreams as we get into adulthood? Why are some people living that dream and others aren't? Why are there so many people depressed and living with wishes or regrets? Did some people get lucky? Was it given to them? Or did they persevere and worked hard for it? The reason is that these 'dreams' left out the part about hard work, sacrifice, dedication, discipline, and all of the other things that success demands from you.

Why was this information left out from us while we were growing up? Was it left out deliberately or not? I can speculate all day on why we don't learn the essential skills of adulthood, but that would be a different book. After graduating, whether from High School or College, that is the point most people stop their education. You finish High School with the basics, and you finish college with a little more knowledge on a particular subject. What about everything outside of that? Why don't we seek to obtain more enlightenment? That is the exact thing that happens to many people; they don't take the time to further their knowledge. Those who continue on the path of self-education are often the ones who become the success stories that their old classmates will talk about. You know, the stories you hear about people knowing someone from way back. The person then went on to do something different continued to learn and work on themselves while others stopped somewhere along the way.

I'd bet that it's a higher percentage of people who earned their success than those that had it handed to them. The ones who earned it take responsibility for things that happen to them and adapt to whatever life throws their way; they possess an internal locus of control. The unhappy make excuses and blame their misfortunes on any and everything besides themselves. Everybody will face trials and tribulations throughout life, but the outcome is based on your reaction to it. Are you going to take defeat, or are you going to fight back for what you want? You can only lose so many times before you eventually win. A winning spirit is persistent no matter how bad you are beaten down or how high the odds stacked against you. This is when believing in yourself comes into play—believing that everything will smoothen itself out over time, and you'll get from it whatever you put in.

It is a mindset that you have or you have to develop over time. Either way, it is required for you to have long-lasting success. You must decide that you want better, and you must always look at life's happenings as lessons and look for what you can take from it. You should learn to find happiness in any situation. Money and the things it can buy are just a bonus to your efforts. If you are genuinely happy for others' success, seeing them motivates you to achieve your goals. This type of thinking comes naturally to some, while others focus on developing it over time. There is no right or wrong way. Consistently applying the right emotions and responses to life happenings, learning not to see the bad in obviously unfortunate situations will spearhead your journey in the right direction. I can't stress enough that we are responsible for our happiness and success. On numerous occasions, I have been told that I should give up and focus on my career inside of a company where I was just a number. The so-called "advice" flew right over my head. If I had listened, I would have never written this book, built my online course, started my podcast, or anything else that I have achieved wouldn't even have been possible.

On the other hand, the unhappy and unsuccessful look at everything as bad luck or find an excuse as to why they can't get further than where they are. These people are the same ones who look at people who have nice things or have reached success in their careers or people who are rich as either bad people, just lucky, or sold their soul for the success they have achieved. STAY AWAY FROM THESE PEOPLE!!! This is their way to rationalize their lack of effort and success in their own right. Not everybody will have the same mindset or even be interested in changing their way of thinking, and that's okay. Being cautious and aware of the energy you allow in your life is your way of protecting yourself and safeguarding your peace of mind. Guard yourself against those who aren't giving you the right energy, all they'll do is drain you. This negative mindset comes from a lack of knowledge and self-awareness, being stuck, and feeling like you have no options. If you are that person, or you want to help that person in your life. They must first become aware that there is light at the end of the tunnel and decide to take control of their life. These are steps that no one can force you to take; they have to happen because you want them to. A change in habits and principles is required to switch to the other side of the fence. Trust me, switching over is hard when you have lived your entire life with this way of thinking, but it's not impossible.

Changing Your Habits

We are creatures of habit. Think about things we are told to obey as a child. I'll use the school system as an example; by the time you were in Middle School, you were programmed to the "school system," which was due to habit. The best way to break a habit is not by trying to forget it but by creating new habits to replace the old ones. It can be challenging at first, especially when you are replacing lifelong habits. Your personal growth is going to require discipline for you to create many new habits over time. As soon as you are comfortable, you'll develop a new thought process that will challenge you and require your habits to change. This process feels like working out, it's hard in the beginning, but the more you do it, the easier it becomes. When you are creating new habits, the people close to you will notice. Some will understand and others won't, you'll lose some friends and gain new ones. Remember to stay on track despite what everyone else thinks. Besides, this is your life, and you want the best for yourself. If you are tired of being stagnant and doing the same thing for years and getting the same results, you owe it to yourself to shake things up a bit and get on a new path. Don't you think you deserve to transform into a better version of yourself? The one that you've always "dreamed" about. Well, let's make that dream a reality. The way you do that is by waking up out of that dream and developing a new you. Breakaway from those bad habits that have held you back for so long; time lost cannot be redeemed, so use yours wisely. Don't be so stuck in your ways that you won't admit that the time for change is now.

Some of the things that we gravitate towards, good or bad, come from our comfortability level. Our comfort comes from our habits and familiarity with something. Shifting to go in a different direction takes a while. Compare it to trying to turn a huge cruise ship that's already in motion. That shift is gradual and will happen slowly—no difference in shifting your habits. Changing your habits requires time and consistent application of the new habit you'd like to put in place. You are already moving at full speed, so a sudden shift will not be feasible, the curve happens slowly. Imagine an 18-wheeler speeding at 100MPH, but all of a sudden the driver notices he needs to make a sharp turn, that sharp turn is close to impossible at your current speed. Can you imagine a big rig going that fast and trying to make a sharp turn out of nowhere? I don't know about you, but I see a disaster happening. It is no different from changing into a new habit, it is planned and happens gradually. It comes after you consistently apply yourself to implement this new habit. I have yet to meet someone who has formed any habit, bad or good, by doing it once. Consistency reflects in the definition of habits, "a settled or regular tendency or practice, especially one that is hard to give up." I say that to say, start today. Every day counts when it comes to your growth, and the habits you possess are key drivers for continuous growth. I'm telling you now, you'll be uncomfortable, uncertain, and even have resistance. Stick in there because these are all good signs. If you are familiar with drug abuse, this is the equivalent of an addict going into withdrawal. It's your body telling you that it wants to revert to what it is accustomed to. Fight that desire until it is no longer there.

Importance Of Belief

"If you stand for nothing, you'll fall for anything." We've all heard this saying numerous times. Without any belief, there is no purpose for your life. If you believe in nothing, you'll have nothing to work for; your life will never be fulfilling. It is the equivalent of playing football with no downs or goal line. It is crucial to believe in something, especially if you expect to overcome any obstacle. Believing in yourself and the fact that you can control the outcome of your future is the starting point of believing. It always begins in the mind, "if you can dream it, you can achieve it." This statement carries truth with it; everything you see and use today is the product of someone's imagination. People may have thought they were crazy, but they believed in their vision. These inventors saw things in their heads and made it a reality for the world to see. If all of these things can become a reality, just imagine what you can do if you believe in yourself and put your all into achieving whatever it is that you choose to pursue. Life has no limits; the only limitations that exist are those you place on yourself.

If indeed you don't believe in yourself, no one else will. People can read you when you have not said anything; your energy speaks louder than words. Sometimes what you don't say can say a lot. The most important question is, do you believe in yourself? All of the adversities that are sure to come your way, all of the doubters and tests that will test you in ways you can't imagine. Do you believe deep down inside that you can overcome it all and not lose faith in yourself? Life isn't easy by any means. Many people break the moment they are faced with a challenge and continue to run away from challenges. That is because they don't believe they have what it requires within them to overcome these obstacles. I can assure you that there are millions of people who have faced far worse than what you are faced with, and they were able to overcome and became victorious in their efforts. So I want to ask you, what did these individuals have that you don't have? The difference is, they believed in their dream and their ability to make it a reality.

I wasn't always a believer. I loved finding explanations to rationalize my failures or lack of doing anything. I'd find an excuse for my inability to persist in any of my efforts. I would do these things unintentionally. I was so used to giving excuses that it seemed normal. One day I sat down and was upset with myself for feeling stuck. That very moment I made myself accountable for my success. I committed to everything I set out to do. I would do everything in my power to make things happen; if I didn't have the resources required, I'd find a way around it. If I didn't have the money, I'd work with what I had. At the end of the day, everything worked out in my favor. I would eventually achieve what I set out to achieve, and I would also learn a new skill or lesson in the process. Believing in myself was the most important thing I'd ever done. Now I know there is nothing in this world that I can't achieve, and I mean NOTHING. When you believe in yourself, you may appear cocky to those who don't believe in themselves or don't believe that they can do whatever it is in this world that they desire. Never allow those who don't believe in themselves, make you second guess the belief you have in yourself.

Self-limiting beliefs

We all have self-limiting beliefs for one reason or another. Some may be valid reasons, but you must shake that thinking if you want to improve. We are all guilty of saying them to ourselves. They more often than not begin with "what if," "but I," "I don't," and my favorite of all, "I can't." A high percentage of statements following any of these phrases is a self-limiting belief that you just have to get over. The only way to get over them is by taking action. When I say action, I mean commit to something and doing it 100%. That "what if" or "I can't" will turn into "I did." This process will strengthen you, build your character, and equip you with a new set of tools to add to your toolbox for your future use. Your confidence level will shoot through the roof; you'll look back and be amazed at yourself. You were able to do this amazing thing that you thought was impossible. I never thought I could write a book, look at you reading words that I've personally composed. Once we make it a habit to overpower our old brain, the world will open up in ways we could never imagine.

It is much easier to find an excuse and just stop right there. What if you told yourself that you could and think about what there is to gain. Do you know how the world of possibilities and opportunities would open up for you? You can't be your setback, which is what happens to a lot of people; they talk themselves out of the race before they even get to the starting line. They begin to compare themselves to someone else, not realizing that it isn't a race. It is a journey, and in this journey, no two people will take the same route or have identical challenges that they are faced with. You owe it to yourself to have a prodigious belief in your ability. Take a moment and look into a mirror, now ask yourself, "What can I not achieve?" Your answer should always sound like, "Not a damn thing!!!"

USING FAILURE AS MOTIVATION

You fail the moment that you quit or give up. Success in anything is attainable if you don't lose enthusiasm and you keep going after facing failure. Failure is an opportunity to restart wiser, more focused, and more encouraged. I failed multiple times with my first business before creating a plan that I could finally execute to catapult me to the next level. This failing effort was happening over the years, and I didn't realize it. Once I caught up, I didn't get discouraged. I stepped back and looked at everything from a different perspective and rearranged my approach. I've read many top-tier entrepreneurs' profiles, those that founded some of the biggest brands and companies today. There is a failure, sometimes multiple failures that they had in their life before finding success. Each failure was an awakening that caused them to have thick skin and an edge over others that did not fail. Everything is so accessible nowadays. You can read books; people are open about their journey and tell you their failures to help you avoid making the same mistakes that they made. They went through the trial and error stages for you not to make the same mistakes; that's the point of sharing their story. They want you to know that their success didn't happen overnight. Some people understand that the journey is difficult, and they are willing to help in any way possible. They need to welcome new persons to the billionaire club; they're waiting for YOU.

Keep in mind that to get further and achieve your dreams, you must take action. Some people are so scared to fail that they never get past the stage of planning and dreaming. In the process of taking action, you will run into challenges. You'll do one of two things, figure it out, or you'll get stuck like a deer in the headlights and get hit. You can get hit, but make sure you get back on your feet much wiser. Getting back on your feet or continuing to lay there and feel sorry for yourself will separate the winners from the losers. Pausing or slowing down beats quitting altogether. I've paused and slowed down multiple times, but I have never quit. There are times when quitting is the wise option; just make sure you know the difference between when to quit and when to keep trying. You should never continue doing something that results in something negative just because you don't want to quit. When I say never quit, I mean never quit something because it is too hard or you lack knowledge and capacity, or things of that nature. There are obvious reasons for quitting, such as something that is harming you. For example, if you have something that is damaging you in any way, you should let go. If you aren't feeling fulfilled in your current career, make an exit plan, and leave. You have only one life, and you don't want to live with regrets. There are certain things we should walk away from just to protect ourselves.

No Better Teacher Than Failure

These two things will teach you lessons, success and failure. Success can be deceiving because you can become successful accidentally and not learn any of the lessons you should have learned along the way, which is very dangerous. Some people stumble upon something good and don't possess the mental capacity to retain their newly acquired assets. On the other hand, failure is education and an opportunity to reflect on what you've done wrong and what you need to change to get different results. You will carry these lessons with you throughout your whole life; this is your story. It is expected for people to fail while attempting something out of the ordinary. It is very rare for you to get it right on your first try. Never be afraid of failing. Failure has a bad reputation; people look at it as embarrassing or disgraceful. It can only become disgraceful if you allow failure to become permanent. If you continue to move forward, it is not a failure. Often, we are surrounded by people who don't understand the concept of failure and will make you feel like you are a failure because of their past experiences where they failed and quit. You are a different animal; you eat failure and get stronger.

Michael Jordan failed many times before becoming a champion, but do we look at him as a failure? No, he kept going until he succeeded. Don't even think about saying, "He's Michael Jordan; he's one of the greatest athletes on earth." Before he became famous, he was unknown. Everybody starts at the bottom and works their way up. Are you going to remain grounded, or will you levitate? The only difference is deciding to start and deal with the hard times now, not run away. After being scared and running away from everything, I decided to take a different approach and face my fears head-on.

After this decision, I looked at life differently after every failed attempt. I'd look for ways I could have prevented that failure. Some things are out of your control, and they just happen; other times, you could have prevented your failure; either way, there is a lesson to be learned. The key to learning from failure is identifying the diamond in all the irritation, disappointment, and defeat that you feel at that moment. Once this is done, you are taking control of your emotions. I remember going into a street fight with confidence, just to get knocked on my ass. It was shocking because I had so much confidence going in, and that confidence quickly dropped once I hit the ground. When you hit that concrete, you must get back up and figure out a different approach in a fight or in pursuing your dreams. It can be embarrassing, but what's more embarrassing is you laying there giving up and not giving it another attempt. You must develop the heart of a lion in the moment of disappointment and be ferocious in your subsequent efforts. People will always respect those who fail publicly and continue to fight and eventually prevail. The underdog story is always the best. Hearing and seeing someone come from nothing to something or failure to succeed is what is loved in this world. To be that next success story, you must not give up on yourself.

Once you quit once, it becomes a habit, and you will quit another thing without thinking twice. If you've gotten this far,

I am willing to bet my bottom dollar that you are not a quitter; you are someone who wants to and will go far in life. You are like me and know that you have more to gain than to lose, so you keep going no matter what. You can never say you've failed at something as long as you are still going at it. You can have many failed attempts and never actually fail. When you fail, you get back up immediately and get at it with a new set of skills and more drive. Do you call a champion a failure because he loses one game? Your life is the same way; we are all players in this game called life. We will win, and we will lose, and many times we may lose more times than we'll win. Those wins that we obtain will bring the best feeling in the world and make all of the losses well worth it. Do yourself a favor and become a star in your life because no one else will take those losses for you.

Take "Can't" Out of Your Dictionary

Is there someone I can reach out to who can remove the word "can't" from all human dictionaries (all languages on earth). There are obvious things humans "can't" do, such as: tell me what happens when we die or figure out if the chicken came first or the egg. I'm talking about the things that we can control; our future, our points of view, our beliefs, and what our lives will turn out to be. I once had someone tell me that I wouldn't be able to change the world because it is hard and only famous people can do that, and I needed all of this mega-power to do so. I'd like to steal a line from one of my idols, Jay-Z, and tell that person that, "I'm different, I can't base what I'm gon' be off of what everybody else isn't"(Song: So Ambitious). I will create my legacy, work extra hard to prove people wrong, and, most importantly, prove to myself that I can do anything in this world. Whatever happened to those childhood teachings of being whatever you wanted to be? Was it all just a saying that they thought sounded like a nice thing to say? As we got a little older, we'd hear, "be realistic." If someone ever told you that you couldn't do something, I'm here to tell you that you can do anything you decide to do. Many people are scared to envision a life outside of the norm. The limits they place on themselves are as far as they'll go. If you set a goal and reach it, you will remain there if you choose that; this is it. I've attained my goal. We don't look past what we perceive as our limits. Where I come from, we are told that the options are quite limited; we either die young, play sports, be a drug dealer, become a criminal, or at best good enough to get a mediocre job. I can't recall anyone coming in telling me that I could do anything in this world. The message was always, go to school, get a good job, and retire. The idea of being an entrepreneur, business owner, or anything else that would allow us to choose our limit was non-existent. I believed this and would talk myself out of things by saying, "I can't do that."

That thinking stopped once I was introduced to music videos in the early days of the internet. I was now being introduced to people who looked like me and lived a lifestyle I never knew was possible. That phrase, "I can't," then became, "what if," then "how could I." As I grew older, I opened up to the idea of being a business owner. I didn't know much about it, but I did want the lifestyle I saw on TV. At that point, I had already been selling things at school for extra money, so in a sense, I was already practicing being an entrepreneur and just didn't know it. As the years went by, I became more business savvy and started to understand the process of being your own boss. All preconceived ideas of working hard and retiring went out of the window. Thanks to Hip-Hop, I now felt like I had a chance, and I no longer said, "I can't" I now looked for, "How can I." This opened up a world of opportunities for me.

One Thousand No's For One Yes

I used to take it personally when someone told me no. I'd think they didn't like me or I was being discriminated against, or any other reason I can think of that could justify me being told no. I was like this for most of my life, and I had never pursued beyond that. If someone told me no, I'd stop there and never look for other opportunities. I am a firm believer that everything happens for a reason. We may not see the reasoning in the midst of being rejected or facing a hard time in our lives, but trust me, the future holds something much better in-store. The way you envision things happening for you is rarely the way they come to fruition. Imagine how your life would look if everything went the way you had planned. Life wouldn't have any purpose or challenge to make the rewards that much better. You'd expect things and feel entitled to everything.

Being told no builds thick skin; it prepares you for the realities of the harsh world that you will face. How do you handle rejection? Are you eager to collect those hundreds or thousands of painful No's just to get that one refreshing Yes? Are you willing to go on a losing streak or lose everything? That is what happens sometimes, you may lose it all, but the bounce back from that loss is much greater. In those dark times, you may not see the light, but know that the sun must come out eventually. I was told "No" most of my life. I heard that word so much that it didn't bother me too much as I became an adult. I had become immune to it. I was so used to it that I was surprised when I did receive a yes, even in situations that I was likely to get a yes. Whatever you desire is on the other side of all those no's you are yet to get. If you are persistent, it is impossible to continue to receive no as an answer. How many times have you been told "No" in your life? I bet more times than you've been told "Yes." That is a part of living; you won't always get the answers that you want. When you tell a kid "no," they don't ever comprehend and go away as you'd hope. They persist and continue to ask for whatever they want, or they always find their way back to where they were just rejected. As we begin to understand life a little more, we were told and made to believe that no means no. You hear it from your parents, your teachers, and many other authorities in your life. Is this why we aren't as persistent with our efforts compared to when we were children? As we get older, we begin to think that being told no is a bad thing or that it is the end of the road in our efforts.

When in actuality, it is an opportunity for us to approach life from a different angle and take a road that may be a better choice for us in the long run. Being told no is just a way of rerouting you in the right direction. Not many people can handle rejection; many feel embarrassed, sad, or allow getting rejected to lower their self-esteem. In my mind, everything that happens in life is perception. If you perceive being told no as a bad thing, then that's what it'll be. On the contrary, if you look for the good that can come from it, then its dynamic changes. Don't allow yourself to be a victim of your self-limiting beliefs; challenge yourself to discover the good in the bad.

HAPPINESS LIVES WITHIN

What is happiness to you, and how does a happy life look for you? Better relationships, better health? These things are all person-specific. For a very long time, I walked around unhappy and didn't even know it. It was happening in my unconscious mind, so everything seemed pretty normal. As I got in tune with myself and became more enlightened about personal development, I realized that I was not happy. My mood swings and moments of daydreaming became obvious to me. I would catch myself complaining and finding a problem with any and everything. I was searching for happiness in the wrong places, which felt like pouring into a bottomless glass. I'm glad that I took note of this behavior, this enlightenment was a life-changer, and I needed it to reach my fullest potential and find my purpose. As I mentioned earlier in the book, I began doing extensive research on personal development. During my research, I realized that the way I thought about happiness was all wrong. I always worried about the wrong things, the irrelevant things, that held no value. Instead, I needed to focus on the inner me, my growth, and the tasks in front of me. I'd always find myself dwelling on my past and being hard on myself about things I did or didn't do. When in reality, I needed to learn from those experiences and make better choices right now. The very moment I understood this, I began to make better decisions and shifted my focus towards the things that would help me at the moment. Being in the moment is where I needed to be. Being there, I could give 100% of my attention and energy to the task in front of me. Doing so left little room for my mind to wander off into those areas that would give me feelings of guilt, doubt, and curiosity.

In this process, I realized that happiness is a decision you make; it comes from within. Happiness comes from continuous actions towards things that will benefit from your gain, which is person-specific. It is a feeling that you'll have whether you were poor and went rich or the other way around. The moment this became clear, my happiness grew substantially. Seeing life in this new light was satisfying and refreshing. It gave me clarity on life and more confidence to achieve the big goals that I always had. I say to you that you must find your internal peace; it is where you will find your true happiness. While the outside sources will be satisfying, that is a short-lived moment of joy. Dig deep, and discover your true happy place. You'll feel it the moment it comes to you. The best way to explain this is that it feels refreshing, like an awakening of some sort.

If you are facing hard times, how can you smile? This may be the burning question in your heart. I can't pay my rent, can't pay my phone bill, and just lost my job, and these problems are constantly presenting themselves. It can be tiring living on the hamster wheel, I hear you. I've lived through these moments, and I am here now to give you my testament to overcoming these adversities. When you are in the middle of situations like this, you must truly believe. I mean, come to peace and know that you possess everything within you to come out on top. Dig deep down and bring out that person that you've always dreamed of. It's tricky because we will naturally talk about our current status, which may not be the best. Speaking on it constantly only allows those circumstances to recur. The key to experiencing change is to visualize yourself in a better situation and manifest it in your mind first. Restrain yourself from speaking about the negatives and focus on the results you want. Of course, you don't want to be where you are, and your way out is to take a different approach than you've taken previously. We are faced with hard times to test our willingness to trust ourselves and to push us to the limits we always admired in others. Once the dust settles and you are still standing tall, that will be your proof and a confidence builder for you to realize your inner strength. All obstacles are temporary as long as you keep going. There was a point in my life where I had to overdraft my bank accounts the same day I got paid just to survive. Those days are long gone. I am living proof that nothing can hold you back. Even in those times, I found reasons to smile and not allow those circumstances to define who I am as an individual. I knew that it was all temporary, but only if I changed my habits. I wanted to be truly happy, so I forced myself to be uncomfortable for a moment and sacrificed my current pleasures for long-term growth.

Benefits Of Being Happy

Being happy changes everything around you. It will attract all the right things and people into your life, and there is a different glow that you give off. You get back what you put out. The Law Of Attraction is real. I know this because I've experienced it. When I was stressed and depressed, I had negative vibes around me, and nothing ever happened in my favor. My bad days were really bad, and good days didn't seem to exist; it felt like I was just flowing with the tide. The moment that I changed my thinking, everything else in my life just seemed to line up. My days were much brighter, and I stood with a little more pride. I walked around with an aura around me that others would see and feel instantly; my vibrations were now on a different wavelength. I'm not telling you anything I haven't witnessed or experienced myself.

Trust me when I tell you that you get from the world what you put out. Believe in yourself and the universe, and watch amazing things happen right in front of your eyes. A genuine smile can cure so much pain that we tend to hold in. We hold the power of the universe within us, and that power is on display when we are truly happy. Anytime something negative pops in your head, it is your responsibility to reject it. The moment you allow it to take over your mind, and you begin to think negatively, you have been defeated. I can't stress it enough that everything manifests in your mind; then it becomes your reality.

The majority of the American population is unhappy, and many don't know why. They don't know how to soul search and get in touch with themselves so that they can find the root cause of their unhappiness. Don't worry if you are in that space; I have your back. We're about to dig and find that happiness together. Would you agree that everyone deserves happiness? Besides, life was meant to be lived and loved, no matter your situation. Whether you are striving to get out of poverty or a single mother doing your best to provide for your kids, it is your right to be happy. Yet, the obstacles that are thrown at us sometimes make us feel the complete opposite. It feels like we are in the worst possible situations at the worst possible times - Murphy's Law. You feel this way because no one has prepared you for these unfortunate events. The feeling of life being unfair or the daunting rhetorical question "Why me?". We weren't taught that if we give energy to the negative, then that is what we'll continue to reap. What if I told you that you could change your circumstances by changing your pattern of thoughts? That's right, the moment you give energy to something, it will appear in your reality. Of course, it takes more than thinking about it. You have to do the hard work that is required. Some things may take a little longer than others, but they will appear. If you had a bad encounter and tend to dwell on it, you will continue to experience similar situations. On the contrary, if you are not bothered by it, acknowledge it, and allow it to pass and direct your energy to a positive cause, the negative will disappear. It is incredible how powerful our minds and energy can be when they're aligned and used correctly.

Let's identify the last time you were truly happy? I'm talking about walking down the street with a smile, not fazed by life's mishaps. How did it feel? Why were you happy? More importantly, can you remember when your happiness started to deteriorate? What event took place? Did anyone or anything come or go in your life? Take some time to write these questions down along with their answers. This is going to be the basis for restoring your happiness. Building a timeline for your shifts will arm you with the ammunition you need to win this battle. I will cover some of the most common factors that lead to unhappiness and provide solutions to these problems. You will surely get what works for you.

Remove All Toxins

There are things in our lives that we must remove so that we can achieve our ultimate happiness. Let's start the process of elimination. If you feel that another person is the cause of your unhappiness, do me a favor and remove that person from your life. When I say remove, I don't mean cut them off completely unless they are very toxic. I mean, start to change the way you communicate with them, the amount of time you spend together, and stop being that sounding board or helping hand you've been to them. I think you get where I'm going with this. Basically, draw a bridge between the two of you, but don't burn the bridge; just remove a few steps from the path for them to get to you. Having toxic people around can be draining; it can wear you down mentally, and you will become stressed or depressed, and you won't even know why. Toxic people come in many disguises; they can be your neighbors, co-workers, spouse, friends, or maybe even your family members. These are the people that are always complaining, gossiping about others, or finding fault with something or someone. The day can be going perfectly fine; then here they come with the negative toxins oozing from their pores and wearing you down with them. The energy that they give off is not the type of energy that helps you excel; it is the kind that drains your mood. It may not always be people; your surroundings can also cause this. You must be aware of what is draining your energy and not giving you that jolt of motivation required to live a healthy lifestyle. We all have had them at some point in our lives. You can only blame yourself for keeping something or someone that drains you close by. Stay away!

Finances

Many people feel that most of their problems will be solved or life would be easier if they had more money. With that being said, many adults have no financial literacy; even if they had more money, they would probably mishandle it and continue repeating the same cycle. Even worse, many adults have no savings account or funds set aside for emergencies. Living expenses today in most major cities in the US are ridiculously high compared to the wages, making it close to impossible to save. I've been there, I've lived paycheck to paycheck, had massive debt, and my money was spent before it even hit my account. I knew that there was a better way of living; I knew that I wanted to do better, but how to do so seemed out of reach. I got fascinated with wealth building in my late twenties. I always understood what it was but never knew how it worked in real life. So I went on a quest to find out all that I could about financial freedom, from assets vs liabilities, trusts, tax loopholes, and a lot more dealing with the subject. Learning about it was both motivating and eye-opening; there was so much to the subject that seemed to be hidden, at least for me since no one I knew was aware, let alone mentioned it. All I heard was, "graduate from high school and get a good job with benefits." I can't expect someone to teach me something that they don't know themselves. So self-education was my key to becoming financially literate and breaking a lifelong cycle of living from hand to mouth.

Educating yourself is one of the best things you can do, especially when it comes to your finances. Budgeting is crucial; it takes so much self-discipline to stick with a planned budget, it can be tempting to spend on things you want, especially when you have the money or credit to do so. Money makes the world go round is a pretty famous saying. This statement is true for some and false for others. Let me explain. For those who grew up without money, it seems that all of our problems are money-related. We don't learn to base our feelings on the things that money can't buy. From the time we are children, we are denied things because our families couldn't afford them. Once we grew into adulthood, became credit-worthy, got a job, and made our own money, we then feel the power of the dollar. We can now purchase things, and it becomes a habit, sounds familiar? Even going as far as damaging our credit. We'll find ways to rationalize our reckless spending. This way of living becomes addictive and is a tough habit for many to break. If you can't manage $1,000 or $10,000, how do you expect to handle more? You will learn things growing up in these conditions that will help you in life if you utilize them correctly. For example, you will learn survival, learn how to make money, stretch, and have thick skin to the world's cruelties. There are countless lessons that I am grateful for learning because I grew up broke. Sometimes, growing up with money, you learn a different set of values. You learn the value of investing, saving, the importance of good health, and many more values that money can't buy. You learn the importance of ownership, assets vs liabilities, protecting money, and wealth creation. Having these values serve as an advantage over those who grew up with a shortage of money. There are always pros and cons to all circumstances. These statements aren't true for all, but as a whole, the percentages will lead in this direction.

Ok, DJ, how can I fix this? Don't worry; I have a solution for you. If you did grow up in an environment where money wasn't always there, it would take retraining of the mind. There is a habit that has to get overturned. You have to want to change your situation. Let me warn you now; it will be difficult for many depending on how bad you want it and how fed up you are with your situation. First, you have to define your financial goals, whether achieving a specific credit score, building wealth, a nice amount of cash in your bank account, paying off debt, or a combination of multiple things. Now that we have the goal set, LET'S GO!

Disclaimer: I am not a financial advisor at all. I am just sharing things that have worked for me.

Why is this goal important to you? What is your reason for wanting this? You will need a strong enough why, a great desire to light a fire in you until it is done. Next, create a spreadsheet with your daily, weekly, and monthly spending. Did you see anything that you can cut back on? Do you eat out, have drinks, can you carpool to work? Look for anything that you can remove immediately. Start by cutting back on any unnecessary expenses that you can live without. This will free up some extra cash for you to put towards your financial goal. What about shopping? Can you buy a cheaper brand? Find something that will last longer for less money? Can you get it from a 2nd hand store? Or just stay in so that you aren't presented with opportunities to shop. Removing these small things will make a big difference in the long run. Open separate savings account that you won't touch, something that's not linked to your primary bank account, and start by putting in $50 a week or whatever you can afford. You will act as if this money doesn't even exist. If you have a direct deposit, go into your payroll and set up for this $50(or whatever amount you can afford) to go into this separate account and keep the rest for your primary account. Let's put those credit cards away. Their high-interest rates will drain you; trust me, I know. Instead, keep a $100 bill as an emergency fund. Suppose there is something that you want to purchase for yourself, set up a different fund for that, and put money away so that you'll be able to purchase it without disrupting your budget. While this won't increase your income, it will teach you discipline.

Increasing Your Income

One of the first things you should do if you are looking to increase your income is to pay off debt. Identify all of the small bills that take those small portions of your income every month; you know the ones that seem like they never go away. I tackled my debt by paying off my smallest balances first. I'd write all of my bills down and write down the minimum amount next to them. I'd then add them up and subtract the sum of all of my debts and bills from my monthly income. The extra that I had leftover would go to the lowest balance. Once that debt was paid off, I'd add that minimum payment to the following debt on the list. Once my debt was down to a more manageable point, I felt a big weight lifted off my shoulders. I then felt that I could do a lot more and focus on advancing myself personally. I had never understood the importance of credit until I needed it for important things. I now watch my credit with a close eye.

There are many ways to increase your income, which stares at you in the face every day. If you are looking to make a little more money in the short-term, know that you aren't too good for anything you can tolerate. One of the quickest ways to make quick money is to sell your unwanted stuff. Yes, you'll get less than what you paid, but it's better than it sitting there collecting dust and continuing to drop in value. Get money for it now before it gets so old that no one even wants it for free. There are so many platforms that allow you to post a picture with a price, and magic, there's a call or text from an interested party and money in your pocket. You can drive part-time for a ride share service. This takes energy and the willingness to deal with different personalities, traffic, and having patience overall. Are you good at math, English, or any other school subject? Become a tutor; tutoring can eventually be scaled into a lucrative business if you market it right. People are always willing to pay money to ensure that their kids are performing well in school. The last thing a parent wants is their child getting ridiculed because they are falling behind in school. Imagine if you charge $75 a week for three days of tutoring. That's an extra $300 a month. What if you had more kids with this same system? That's right, more money for you, think outside of the box. I can go on, but now you understand there are many ways to add to your income. Find something that works for you and your lifestyle. Remember, these little hustles are temporary and are only meant to help you get to the next level until you find something you enjoy doing and can make into a legit business.

There are many ways to increase your income that was not mentioned above. They are just a few suggestions to get your imagination going. Sometimes you have to leave your pride and ego at the door so that you can do things that you wouldn't think about initially. The things you want in the long run will only become possible with the sacrifices you make today. It is a great feeling and accomplishment when you can be financially free. The only way to become so is by making changes today. This is the perfect time to decide to break those bad choices that have been haunting you for years and take control of your financial future. I may not be the most wealthy person globally, but I am more wealthy than I previously was, and it is only growing. That is only possible because I sacrificed so much to get on this path that I'm on. If I did it, you can too. I didn't have anyone there to educate me, so I made mistakes and learned the hard way. I'm giving you things I wish I had learned. Maybe you know, perhaps not, but take what you can use and let the rest go over your head. If you have learned lessons and see someone going down the same path, I ask you to pass the knowledge.

Love Your Life

There is no doubt that life is filled with obstacles; some can tear you down and make you question your faith and existence. Don't beat yourself up; it's normal. We all have had that feeling of whether we are wasting our time or if it'll be best to quit. To beat this feeling, time and time again, requires clarity; you must love your life and love what you do. Whatever you are working on should never feel like work. It is something you look forward to doing; it doesn't feel like a task. You wake up with excitement and enthusiasm; you are looking forward to putting in the work. Even then, there will be a hurdle that will catch you by surprise. It can drain your energy, affect your mood, and have you feeling unproductive or that energy and enthusiasm that you need is absent. Keeping in mind the reason for your journey will allow you to bounce back and regenerate that energy that has just been drained. Loving what you do makes things much easier. We were all put on this earth with a purpose, one that may come sooner or later for some. It takes a lot of life experiences to determine your reason for being on this earth. Some of us may never find that reason; it can become a daunting task for many to discover their "calling." I love guiding people to reach their full potential. Seeing people happy brings me joy. I genuinely believe that everyone should love their journey and, most of all, love the life that they live because there is no better life for them.

STRESS RELIEF

f I could discover the cure for stress, I'm pretty sure my life wouldn't be the same. I don't have the answer for you, so I've decided to provide a few practical steps and tips to ease the tension. When was the last time you were stressed? Was the stressor an unfortunate situation or something that you couldn't figure out? I'm pretty sure we've all been there before. Some of you may be dealing with stress as you are reading this book. It is perfectly normal to have some form of stress from time to time, but it becomes detrimental when it persists for long periods. In my experience, stress is mainly caused by overthinking or focusing on the past or future outcomes of a situation. The stress experienced by an average adult in America is due to financial difficulties, relationships, or work. There are ways to battle this stress that many people never discover.

One of those things is, understanding that it starts in the mind. Once you take control of your thoughts and shift your them to see the good in all situations, you will be on the right track to combating stress. Developing a positive mindset takes practice; the best thing to do is to replace bad thoughts with good thoughts. As soon as you notice the negative ones developing, it will eventually become a habit. It's easy to complain about your problems because you are the one experiencing them. Always remember that there is someone that would trade their problems for yours in a split second. Have you ever experienced a situation that felt like it was the worst thing that could ever happen? Guess what, you survived. That alone should be enough motivation for you to continue to move forward. No matter what you do, you will get stressed. It is your responsibility to learn how to react to stress.

It would help if you had an outlet from stress. Everyone has something that they love, something that's a passion or a favorite hobby. You'd do this thing for free just because you love it. It is crucial to have this thing that you love to counteract the stress that will arise daily. It can be your escape from your stress, while at the same time acting as entertainment or enjoyment. This helps relieve stress and puts you at ease no matter what is going on in your life. It is imperative to have a few things that you can rely on as stress relievers. A few things that do this for me are, Koi ponds, aquariums, and basketball. These are all very personal to me, and each steers me away from whatever stress that I am feeling at any given moment.

I love water naturally, but Koi Ponds and fish tanks are so relaxing and serene for me. They help me calm down, come down to earth, be in the moment, and enjoy life's simple things. I love to watch the fish swim gracefully throughout the water.

I can sit there and watch them for hours. Just the sound of a subtle waterfall and water flowing along with light water splashes always takes me to another world. It reminds me to be free, move freely at my beat, and not get caught in life's web. Aquatic life does not share the same emotions as humans, so their world is different, and they will never show emotion or judge you at all.

For this reason, I find marine life fascinating. I had a few saltwater aquariums, and I loved them all; the fish have so much personality. I looked forward to them swimming towards me when I walked into the house. In my mind, they were greeting me even though I know that they were only looking for food. The point is, they acknowledged me, and that made me feel important no matter what was happening with my day. I could always depend on my aquatic friends to relieve me of any stress I was facing. I've always found water therapeutic, from rain, streams, oceans, even a nice bubble bath. My home will have a Japanese Garden with a waterfall that will flow from the house into the backyard equipped with floating stones, a large shark tank in the main living quarters, and a reef tank inside of my office. Needless to say, it is a must that water features surround me. Water never fails to help me restore my energy and helps me relax. Until that day comes, I make it my mission to seek out a body of water just to have a little time to myself and release whatever is crowding my mind. There is nothing more valuable than peace of mind; no amount of money can replace a stress-free life.

Basketball was my first love. I swore I was going to the NBA; I was good at one point. Life happens, and things don't work out as you planned, and I understood that. The love you have for the game itself will never fade away. Anytime I am on the court, I can zone out and shoot around for hours; I can do this alone or with a group. My mind is focused on the physical things happening, and I am no longer worried about problems outside the lines. Any sports activity requires you to be in the moment. If you find yourself drifting off for too long, you'll quickly get reminded by your opponent coming right at you. As with any high-intensity activity, you are required to be there not just physically but also mentally. It doesn't have to be basketball or a traditional sport; it can be anything that is physical and requires you to be in the moment. I can't name one time that I played basketball while my mind was in another place.

I share these things with you to say, find your inner peace. Something that lifts you no matter what is going on. We live in a busy world where a 15-second unfavorable exchange can cause your whole day to go south. It is healthy and essential to have this escape; it is healthy and necessary for your wellbeing. You can't stop the things you have no control over, but you can find something that'll help you escape from your reality for a brief moment. Escaping will allow you to see things from a different perspective, get your creative juices flowing, and get in tune with yourself. When your mind is filled with junk, you should always have a method to ease your mind. Physical activities are a sure way to ease stress, and breathing exercises work as well. There are thousands of methods for you to use that'll help drop your stress level.

Some people use drugs and/or alcohol for this; I believe that using substances is a way to mask the real problems and sweep them under the rug. You are mature enough to make and be responsible for your decisions if you are eighteen and above. I'm not against alcohol or legal drugs, but you must learn to deal with your problems with a sober mind. You can have your alcohol or whatever you like another time, but you must learn not to rely on these substances to escape your reality or problems. Drugs, alcohol, and other substances weaken your brain, immune system and can have many detrimental effects on your health, making you more vulnerable and prone to foreign sickness or disease. I grew up in an environment where drug use and its effects were a part of everyday life. By the age of 6 or 7, I was used to seeing people that looked like zombies, literally. They would walk around talking to themselves, committing crimes so that they could make money just to buy more drugs. It was horrible, but it was a reality. I knew that I didn't want to do any type of drugs, legal or illegal. I didn't do any better; I became a dealer for a short time to make some pocket change. I also knew that I was becoming a part of the problem, so I stopped.

Have some time to yourself, and decongest your mind, work on your mental state. Apply this to your life to get refreshed from time to time. It'll allow you to approach challenges and situations with a clear, healthy mind. Having a clear mind will help you make smarter decisions. When we go through life without taking breaks from time to time, things will eventually crash. There is only so much that our mind and body can take before it gets overwhelmed. We tend to take our pain and challenges with us and mask it. This build-up is deadly because you will explode, and let's hope that you don't spill on the wrong person or in the wrong situation. The secret is being in control of your emotions, situations, and life. Once you are in full control, you choose which way you go.

A Powerful Routine

Before getting out of bed, I lay in silence and let my mind roam freely for about 5 minutes or so. Then I get up, brush my teeth, wash my face and take 10-15 minutes to meditate. Meditation is a great way to relieve stress, just letting your body go, let your mind roam, and be in the moment. Even if you start with only 5 minutes, something is better than nothing at all. The first hour of my day is the time I take to set the tone for the rest of my day. After meditation, I go over my goals for the day, check emails, work on my big projects, and do some research and social media marketing. This sets the tone for my day; now, I am ready for whatever the day brings because most of my demanding tasks are already complete. I keep myself on a schedule, which I plan out the night before, with a little cushion for unexpected events. Of course, there is no way to prevent the unpredictable, so my most important tasks are already complete if something pops up. I now have the flexibility to shuffle things around.

My days weren't always this organized. I'd wake up whenever I felt like it and get up, scroll on my phone for hours at a time, then do whatever popped up in my head. My day had no structure at all; I'd find time to do things I should have gotten done already at some point in my day. I'd always make myself seem busy just to say that I did something when in actuality, I didn't do anything at all. I'd deprive myself of sleep and put a considerable strain on my body. During the time I was doing this, I had no clue that's what I was doing. I had always heard about the stories of successful people waking up early and making a huge difference in productivity and overall health. To be honest, I thought it was all BS, that's until I gave it a shot myself. Now, I don't recall what made me take it seriously, but whatever it was, I'm glad it registered in my brain. After waking up early consistently, I saw a drastic boost in all aspects of my life.

Waking up early adds hours to your day. While I feel more creative and productive at night, there is something about waking up a little earlier that boosts your progression. You are well-rested, nothing crowding your mind, and you are adding hours to your day. This is especially good for those who have a day job. The early morning routine allows you to wake up and work on your tasks before any dark cloud pollutes your mind. The average day carries a lot of baggage with it that you can't control. The grind of working, dealing with people, traffic, or family can take a toll on you, and you are drained by the time you get home. You'll find yourself putting things off until later because the day beat you up. For readers who believe that "you are a night person," I challenge you to give it a try for two straight weeks; trust me, it'll go by fast. Create a morning routine that suits you and do this consistently. Track your progress and take note of what you get accomplished compared to your productivity at night. Even 30 minutes of consistent work is great; it beats doing 3 hours of nothing. I've heard some people mention that they don't have much time, and I ask them to account for their whole day. This exercise reveals a lot of time that is unaccounted for. Write down what you are doing hour by hour to find your areas of opportunity. We lose track of time we are wasting because we aren't paying attention to our activities. Once we take note of this, then we will be able to manage our time much better. When you manage your time, you are now able to manage your life.

"Me Time"

I'm pretty sure you are amazed at the title of this subheading. Read through this subchapter to find out what it really is and how it can change your life powerfully.

Is it just me, or does it feel like 24 hours is not enough time? It feels like there is never enough time in the day, and your days just go by, and another begins. You can burn out very fast, feeling like you are always doing something. These burnouts can come in many forms, and you may not even know it. If you get agitated very quickly at the smallest things, have frequent mood swings, become frustrated with your kids or people close to you, or forget the simplest things, you might be experiencing burnout. These are just a few symptoms that can indicate that you are overwhelmed and need a break. Sometimes the break you need is mental, not physical. You need time away from everyday life to reconnect with yourself and get back in tune with the high spirit you once displayed. Learning to identify when you are overwhelmed is a great practice to help prevent being taken over completely. This awareness comes with knowing yourself and the threshold you can handle. I know some people who can handle having a career, a family, taking care of the kids, and managing a household. In contrast, someone else is having a hard time with being a student with no kid. The tolerance level is different for everyone. Never listen to, or tell someone what they should be able to handle. They may be dealing with internal battles that you can't see.

You should never doubt or feel bad about finding time for yourself. If you don't do this, everything around you will crumble, and the people around you will feel your rage. Taking time out to reconnect and clear your mind is essential for your well-being. Finding that quiet time to do things you want to do for yourself is golden when it seems you are always on the go. It is one of the main things you can do to help your mental health. Having a little "me time" will be a sure way to keep your balance and not go insane. It is a great practice to schedule your time alone for yourself as much as possible. It is your choice if you choose to allow others to join you in on your detox time. Whatever works for you is the best method; just make sure you are taking a break from your daily routine.

Balancing Life

I fell in love with meditation once I started feeling the balance of energy it brought into my life. Learning about the chakras that human bodies are composed of was a real moment of awakening for my spiritual being. When I meditate, it feels as if

I'm letting go of a lot of stress and starting with a clear mind. I may be feeling a little tense or like my brain is overloaded, but meditation balances and clears out all the clutter. One needs to find balance in life. Balance in all parts of your life is a key ingredient to living a healthy and fulfilling lifestyle. Have you ever tried to balance your weight while walking a tight line? Did you notice that you will wobble while rocking from one side to the other? The longer you walk and balance yourself with your arms, the easier it becomes. After balancing yourself for so long, you uncover the proper weight distribution and find your sweet spot for keeping your balance; as soon as you put your arms down, shaking increases. Life is no different, you can have one part of your life under control while neglecting another, and things begin to get off balance. You must walk that fine line slowly with your arms sticking straight to the side. It helps you find balance, and if you feel yourself tilting, you shift your weight accordingly. It is not uncommon for us to excel in one area in our life and have a very poor performance in others. I've personally done it myself; I'll work on one thing and not put enough energy into others. Sometimes things around us are spiraling out of control, and we don't seem to notice it because we are killing it in another area where we've put all of our focus. Those on the outside looking in can see it happening first hand, whether that be our health, relationships, parenting, or anything else that deserves a fair amount of our attention. It can become worse if you don't notice or acknowledge that you are slacking, but if you own up to it, you have the power to make adjustments and do exceptionally well in all parts of your life and not just one.

You must find a way to take your experiences and use them as an advantage in life. Everyone possesses some type of characteristic(s) that they can use as their advantage. The real challenge is figuring out what that advantage is. To discover it, you must attempt different things in your life. This is how you'll find that edge that you have over the rest of the population. This requires you to step out of your comfort zone and do things you wouldn't have done before. You can become so immersed in your current endeavors that you forget to pay attention to other things and people around you. You may not know it, but those around you and other things you do keep your ability to strive at your maximum level. Look at it as if it's a plant. Giving it too much water or too much sun can damage it. How bad it gets damaged all depends on the care you put into it.

Allocating Your Time

Picture this. You're on a roll, running your business for a little over a year now. Sales are picking up, and you've learned from your past mistakes. Your confidence level is picking up, and you feel like it's time to step up your game. Your life revolves around the business right now. It is your number one priority above anything else. This is looking very promising to help you leave the job that you hate so much. Your spouse has supported your dreams and encouraged you to take the appropriate steps to continue to grow your business. He/She has also been asking that you'd spend more time with the family and pay them a little more attention. It feels like they're the secret relationship, and your business is your main thing to your spouse. You argue that you are doing this to create a better future for the family, and once you get to the destination, the family will have your undivided attention. He/she has been waiting for a while now and is gradually becoming impatient. They want more commitment, but you feel that you don't have time at the moment because you have huge goals to achieve. Sacrificing your time is the last thing that makes sense at this point. Will your significant other be wrong to leave you for someone else that can give them what they want right now?

This story occurs very frequently. Building a business or even yourself from scratch and giving something your complete focus is a huge challenge, and not everyone can do it. It will require a lot of your time, and most times it will take money to build it up before you see a return. You have to be mindful of this before going into business for yourself while others depend on you. Whether they depend on you for time, money, or affection, they are entitled to that attention. In your mind, you may feel like they should understand and see the bigger picture. In some cases, you may become lucky and have someone who does. Most of the time, it is not the case; we are all selfish and look for our interests first, which is not bad. If you found 20 dollars, you won't think about how someone else could spend it. Once you get the tunnel vision, everything else doesn't matter. Sometimes we even neglect ourselves. We forget to take those well-needed breaks to allow our minds to declutter.

Learning to find time is essential to a healthy lifestyle. One simple thing you can do to assist with your time management is keeping a To-Do list. A To-Do list allows you to prioritize things, and you can physically see what needs to get done. This goes along with your daily activities and writing down your goals. Your goals should be ordered from short-term goals to your long-term goals. Now you have some structure in place and can better allocate your time. You can now plan out dates with whom you need to; you can schedule meetings and open up time to network and grow your business and your brand.

Don't Neglect You

You are the main machine. You are the reason that everything in your life is the way it is. We tend to drop ourselves out of our priority list while putting other people and things at the top of it. Most of the time, we don't get the same in return, and we continue not to prioritize ourselves. We are all guilty of this at one point or another. Whether it is expected of you or not, we have all done it or will do it at some point in our lives.

I've neglected myself on many occasions throughout my life. I've been guilty of ignoring my health, finances, even important relationships. I corrected this because I knew that it wasn't healthy and that it would continue to do more harm. I see many people making many of these mistakes I made over the years. The difference is, I stopped, and they are still in the cycle of repeating the same mistakes. I had it bad; I lost so much weight that people thought I was sick; at my lowest, I weighed 113lbs. I was very insecure during this time in my life. People around me noticed it right away. This loss of weight was the result of stress and neglecting myself. I would go a whole day without eating or not eating as much as I needed to eat in order to become a healthy size for my height and age. I'm thin and long, I'm not super tall, but I look much taller because of my long arms and legs plus my slim build. Many people would usually say that I look like I weighed 140-150lbs, and I took that as a compliment. I knew it was getting out of hand and that I needed to take it more seriously. So I began eating and working out more often and developed a routine to gain weight and stay healthy. One misconception people have is that being skinny is being healthy. I tell you assuredly; this is not true!

During this part of my journey, the lesson I learned was that you are responsible for yourself, not your best friend, spouse, or parents, YOU! No one can make you get up and do what's right for you or tell you what you should be doing. The only person that can enforce a change is you, and it begins in your mind. All of the decisions we make are a result of a thought that we first developed or imagined. I envisioned the future me, what I saw myself becoming, and the changes I will need to develop into that person. It began with the small things that I always overlooked. My day-to-day activities had to change, and habits had to change for me to become that person I had envisioned. It is no different with you; visualize where you want to be at your highest peak and work your way into becoming that person. Eliminate things and people that waste your time and balance out your life. You must get serious with yourself and not offer any breaks or excuses.

MEET THE BARKING DOG

I know you are wondering, meet the barking dog? What are you talking about, and where is all this going? Relax, the barking dog I speak of, refers to that voice in your head that keeps stopping you from taking action towards something. You know, the one voice that scares you and keeps you stagnant. It is that imaginary voice telling you that you can't do it or convincing you that it is too hard. How do you know that you can't do something you've never tried? What do you have to lose? In most cases, you have more to gain than to lose. The fear of failing holds people back from ever taking any action. This fear comes from the uncertainty of trying something new. You don't know if you'll succeed, you don't know how people will perceive you, you don't know where to start, and the list goes on and on.

We were all kids at one point, we didn't know how to walk, ride a bike, read, or write, but we learned by trial and error. Every time we failed, we kept trying and got better with every attempt. It's the same with life. The only difference is that we are now nervous and worried about what others may think. It seems that people lose interest in learning new things as they get older. They get content with their mental state and rarely attempt to improve themselves. You will always encounter new situations that you are unfamiliar with, but you must not turn away. You should always tackle these tasks head-on. Time will continue to pass whether you try it or not, so give it your all. What are you going to lose in the process? If what you have to gain outweighs your potential losses, then it should be a no-brainer.

I was scared of the barking dog for many years, and it took me some time to overcome it. I was very shy and didn't want to speak with people. I was insecure; I thought I was too dark, too skinny, what will they think, what if they don't respond the way I want them to? These things would continuously run through my head whenever it was time for me to confront something or someone. Over time, I developed confidence, and in the process, I learned that it wasn't all that bad. You will get some no's, but a yes will eventually come, and that one yes is all you need to build that confidence and reassurance that you must persist. When I used to cold call looking for investment opportunities, I would always tell myself, "It's just a phone call, and what's the worst that could happen?" The worst is they'll just say no and an occasional rant of how they don't want to be contacted again. Those rejections allowed me to develop a thick skin, and I learned to brush it off and go on to the next opportunity. I take that same mentality with me everywhere I go. I walk into a room with confidence because I have everything to gain, and I am going to get all that I want because it's waiting for me to claim it. You should learn to confront that barking dog and show him who's the real boss. Let him know that you've built up the courage to stand up to him, and you will not lose. Once you develop that, everything else will come with ease, and nothing can discourage you, or no one will be able to tell you that you can't do something. You now know that the barking dog isn't the German Shepherd you thought it was, it's just a loud barking Yorkie. We tend to take advice from people who always run away from the barking dog; they eventually live their life running from the unknown confrontations. That's no way to live; you will forever fall short of your full potential if you live like that. We were put here to reach our fullest potential and nothing less. Don't let that barking dog turn you in a direction you don't want to go; if you're going to progress, you'll have to face it eventually. So why not get it out of the way now.

Do you think that your idols knew what would happen every time they started a new venture? I think not. They took risks and sometimes were unsuccessful in their attempts, but they never failed because they persisted and kept going. They may have failed at a task, but not on reaching the goal. They picked themselves up and kept moving with more knowledge. That journey will build character and strength if you are willing to keep going. Don't allow the unknown to scare you away from something you're yet to try. When was the last time you tried something and didn't know what the outcome would be? Was it as bad as you thought? Peradventure it was, I'm pretty sure you learned from it and grew as an individual and can do it again with more knowledge and succeed. That's life; you'll continuously face obstacles that will challenge you; it's all about taking on the challenge. That fear may come from past experiences, or maybe others not believing in you, making you question your abilities. These are all true if you choose to let them define you. If you decide to become much more than what you're labeled, that barking dog will slowly become muffled.

Get Out Of Your Way

Often, we doubt ourselves and our abilities, or even work very hard and feel that we've done nothing at all. Being hard on ourselves is something that most of us do; we tend to overthink things and make them worse than they are. We will incur many self-limiting beliefs that we place on ourselves for no apparent reason. They can be so strong that you begin to believe them. Doing so is pernicious. It's like inoculating yourself a disease without knowing that it is a disease. You are inflicting yourself and putting a ceiling on your growth. This imaginary ceiling will no longer exist when you come to your senses and start believing in yourself. Anybody who has accomplished a goal, large or small, had to overcome that voice in their head. This voice sounded convenient, pleasurable, or even convincing. Living in the moment will keep you in the cycle of repeating the same results. Break out of that cycle by any means possible. You'll do yourself a favor by becoming aware of your self-inflicting harm.

Understand that you hold the key to your destiny; you are in the driver's seat of your life. The moment you allow the doubts to penetrate your head, you are giving up control. It may get so strong that you won't realize that you are putting yourself inside of a prison in your mind. If you can admit to this, great, you are aware and can now consciously change for the better. The scary part is when it begins to happen unconsciously, and you can't control it. You are no longer in control of your mind; you've become a slave to your thoughts. You must take back control of your mind and become the driver and navigator again, don't sit in the backseat as a passenger, letting whatever happens just happen. Taking control means that you can make the necessary adjustments while on this journey of life. If you remain a passenger, you'll never reach your desired destination. While we are the ones in control of our destiny, on the contrary, we are also our own worst enemy. Beat yourself, and you win. Our minds are very powerful and are there to protect us from danger. This danger is determined based on our beliefs and past experiences. If we've identified something as dangerous, the next time we encounter it we'll automatically go into defense mode. That's just how the brain is wired. The key to beating your mind is to know that you now view an experience or belief differently. You are now tearing down the gates that your mind put in place to protect you. Shift your thinking, and you will shift your results. Most of the time, we are not getting results because we keep trying the things we are comfortable with because our minds are programmed to believe that's the only way. Get out of your head and get moving.

All Fears Are Mental

Fear kills more dreams than failure ever will. Fear will stop you from trying something, but failure will strengthen you to continue to try. The fear of rejection, failure, judgment, the unknown, plus many more can halt your dreams if you allow them to. They are like having an infection; they can all be cured with the right treatment. All fears that we accumulate over time are things that we've never tried most of the time. We are going off of someone else's experience and how that person describes it. Building a false sense of reality on someone else's opinion and not allowing ourselves to experience it and develop our own opinion. When you were little, you'd listen to your parents when they tell you that something is bad for you, and you never attempt to find out for yourself. Those made-up stories about the boogie man that'll get you in the dark and too many others that are synonymous with our childhood. As you get older, you may try things you were told not to and discover that you enjoy it. I'd encourage you to treat everything in life the same way, never take the next person's opinion, always seek your own experience.

The world loves stories about the underdog coming out on top. There is something about the person who has all of the odds stacked against them coming out on top. That underdog didn't get there by pure luck. They always believed and didn't allow anything to get in their way. All of the non-believers and chatter about them were not prevailing in their ear, and it turned into fuel. If they allowed this to get into their mind and began to believe it for even one second, they would have lost. 100% of all fears were removed from their body. One thing I learned growing up in my neighborhood is, even if you're scared, never show it. Not showing that you're intimidated builds your confidence because you'll see that what you were scared of isn't that bad. I want to ask you, what are you scared of? What fears are within you? Once these are identified, ask yourself why you are scared in the first place. Never fear anyone; we all bleed and breathe the same air. Never fear anything; what doesn't kill you only makes you stronger.

MAXIMIZING YOUR PRODUCTIVITY

There is a huge difference between being busy and being productive. The two are often confused with being the same. Being productive is taking action towards your goals or something with substance so that you reach higher heights. Productivity pushes you forward; it can be a mental push or just a step to help you move further in life. Being busy, on the other hand, can be anything occupying your time. Things like being on your phone or just watching TV can be considered as being busy. I always thought that I was productive when I was just busy. I would be busy with pointless tasks, things that weren't helping me move forward. These are things that I could have done in my leisure time, but I would never set boundaries for myself and would often find myself doing things just to say that I'm busy. I could have saved my brainpower and just relaxed instead of doing unnecessary activities. As time passed by, I learned this the hard way. Hours would pass, and I'd be in the same place and hadn't accomplished anything.

Once I realized that these simple 20 or 30-minute tasks were lingering on for weeks at a time, it became evident to me. I was not using my time wisely; I'd always say I'll get to it next time. The next time turned into weeks and months, and I was continuously repeating that cycle. I got fed up with myself one day after noticing people I advised were getting past me and achieving their goals. I said enough is enough, and I changed my habits. No more tomorrow or next week; there is no better time than now. Every second wasted is a second lost. Get it done now, and you don't have to worry about it later. I realized that once I start something, I will more than likely finish that task or be much closer to completing the task. This change made me become more productive and utilize my time much better than I had previously done. When I say that my life changed instantly, I immediately saw the results; I felt more fulfilled and capable of achieving even greater things by merely applying myself.

Take Action

I hate treadmills; they are constantly running but going nowhere. It reminds me of people who would repeat things that didn't work. What are you doing? Get moving; that dream isn't going to build itself and come to you; you have to create your reality. These are words that I had to repeat to myself on multiple occasions. I'd find myself doing the same thing day in and day out but getting nowhere. Until one day, I decided that I've had enough of the same routine and continually repeating the same steps. I decided to take action, not just any action. I decided to take the big action steps that I knew would get me to the next level. As adults, we know what we need to do to get the results we want in life. Sometimes, we don't want to do these things, so we continuously put them off time after time. Look at it as a train, it starts slow, but once its speed and momentum pick up, it becomes hard to stop. We tend to drag and procrastinate on tasks that are meant to help us grow. This lack of action will keep us stuck in this lazy phase. We'll put things off until tomorrow, which turns into next week, and so on. Instead, just do it. I have a quick request (don't just read over this without doing it, you will be doing yourself a great disservice). Stop reading right now and do one small task that you've been putting off; just go and get it done.

I'll be waiting for you to get it done.

Now that you've done it, do you feel better? Is there a weight off your shoulder? Do you feel accomplished and relieved? Whatever feeling you have, I'm sure it's a good one. You deserve to feel this way all the time. Taking action is the only way to guarantee that you will continue to feel this way. Taking action isn't the end; it has to be consistent - you have to show up and do the work every day. By doing so, you are also creating powerful habits; now, getting up and doing the work becomes much easier. The hardest part of anything is getting started. When you first learned to ride a bike without training wheels, the most challenging part was staying on the bike during the first few pedals. After you got going, it was a little easier to balance yourself and keep going.

Life is no different; we begin with the training wheels, getting comfortable with what we're getting into. Now we got the hang of it a little bit and are now ready to graduate. When you first start, you may fall a few times, but you'll get back up. The faster you get up, the faster you progress on your journey down the path. Life is no different than a bike ride. You have bumps you have to go over and obstacles you have to go around, but you keep on rolling. You are always pedaling so that you are moving forward. This is a form of taking action. Some of us reach one goal post and stop; we find comfort here. This is like being a kid, and you stop riding once you find a shaded spot on a hot day. You don't want to get back into the sun, you'll be leaving a comfortable position and risking sunburn, dehydration and you don't know when you'll find another shaded spot. Some people are comfortable with that, and that's ok. However, if you are looking to go beyond the average, you must continue to pedal on to the next tree and not settle.

Visualize Your Reality

Close your eyes and picture where you'd like to be. Some refer to this technique as starting with the end in mind. When you start with the end in mind, you see the life you are working towards today. If it is in your head, it is more likely that you can make it a reality. The only problem I have with this is that so many people fail to realize that your dreams will remain just without the appropriate actions. Visualize, but don't get so caught up in your head that you aren't doing anything to get you closer to that dream. You'll catch yourself daydreaming and fantasizing a little too much and not doing anything to pull you closer to your dream. I use visualizations as a motivator or a method of getting clarity on something I've been stuck on. Visualization should never be used as a crutch or an actual driver to achieving your goals. Dream and visualize, but get to work and create your reality in real life, not just in your head. As part of my coaching program, I encourage my clients to visualize their future, asking them how their future looks? I then ask the follow-up question: how do they envision themselves getting there? Remember that having a vision without a plan will always result in the failure of any venture you choose to pursue. There are always other pieces to the puzzle that we are yet to discover. This discovery only comes with taking action and inching closer towards your desired destination.

Winners Vs. Losers

Whichever side you fall on, it is all inside of your mind. Which side are you on, and what side do you want to be? Don't BS with yourself. You have to take yourself seriously before anyone else does. You are your first fan; the energy you give off, good or bad, will boomerang. You must know that you are already that top-notch person before you reach that level. Let it manifest in your mind, and the body shall follow. This is a skill that all successful people understand. They eventually realize the power of thinking and believing. All champions first envisioned themselves becoming champions before it became a reality. Not only did they envision it, they believed it. If you've ever studied extremely successful people, somewhere in their story, they will mention that, even through all of the struggles and hard times, they believed in their dream before it manifested. Whether you seek a relationship with someone, a new job, business success, or whatever else you can imagine, you must first plant it into your mind.

Losers can have multiple meanings. For this scenario, we are talking about a loser mentality - the feeling of defeat, hopelessness, and putting yourself out of the race before it even begins. We've all encountered losers or have been one before. This form of thinking usually isn't the individuals' fault. It is a result of a series of events taking place over one's life span. There are contributing factors in the household, your friends, your environment, and even the media we consume. When all of these merge, they can have a detrimental effect. This thinking is a disease that could eat you from the inside, but only if you allow it. I was surrounded by individuals infected with this disease; left to them, there was nothing wrong because they didn't know any better. No matter your circumstances, you are the only one who can decide to change it. As a teen and young adult, I was guilty of having a losing mentality. I felt defeated, made excuses, didn't take action, and thought that the world should give me a break because of my upbringing. I was in for a rude shock. Your past doesn't matter; all that matters is what you are doing now to grow and break from your past. I learned how not to let others' criticism about me change how I feel about myself and life. Instead, I would turn it into positive energy and use it as fuel to grow beyond my past and current circumstances. Realizing that these circumstances were all temporary and a stepping stone for me to grow beyond was what kept me afloat. When you aren't presented with winning material, you are more worried about surviving in a losing circle. I'll use poverty-stricken neighborhoods as an example; when you come from this lifestyle, you aren't concerned about creating a better future; you are worried about how you're going to eat right now. You are more concerned with preventing all of the things that could go wrong, and there is no thought for the things that could go right. So the actions you take differ drastically based on you seeing the glass as half empty versus half full.

Opportunity Passes On

You've heard the stories and seen quotes where a company passes up a product or service that eventually became more innovative and changed the game. With these stories, there is always a story of someone passing up the opportunity of riding the wave in its early days. Many times, people and companies spend their time banging their heads because they passed up an opportunity. Many lessons could be learned from these events. One of the most common takeaways would be looking beneath the surface. It is always easy to see things as they appear instead of seeing them as they are or for what they could be. To grow, you must believe in something that no one else has seen at the time. You have that opportunity to decide between letting something pass or hopping on board and riding out the tuff times for a great return. While it does take lots of guts to believe in something that's not guaranteed, it takes even more guts not to take action and remain in the same position a year later. I want you to save yourself, don't think about what could go wrong, but what could go right. If you believe in it why not take action and see the vision through, whether this is your idea or someone else's. Fortunes are always made when someone jumps out of their comfort zone. Like I mentioned earlier, if you are comfortable, you aren't growing, so GET UNCOMFORTABLE. Growth, wealth, and all things great are created when you get out of that comfortable seat and take on a new set of challenges.

Organize Your Life

Are you disorganized, or you know someone who is? They can't seem to find anything, because nothing seems to have place. They frequently use the statement: "I thought I put it right there." I meet these people all the time, and I noticed that if one part of their life is disorganized, it is more likely that more things in their life are disorganized. This can be frustrating to deal with; some people hate it but can't fix it as if their life depended on it. To rationalize, they call it an organized mess. Let me tell you now; there is no such thing as an organized mess. It takes discipline and a willingness to adapt to change. You must first acknowledge the problem and be open to possible solutions.

I've always been an organized person in any space that I occupy. I can tell you where everything is because everything has a place. It allows me to function to my fullest capacity and not waste time looking for things. This comes from years of living this way; as a kid, my mom would make me clean and organize things, which stuck with me. As I grew into an adult, I noticed how being organized helped me get more done and be much more proficient. People will often ask me how I keep everything organized so well, and I will tell them that it's a habit and it comes naturally.

I found out that having an organized mind has a lot to do with achieving things that you set out to accomplish throughout life. Many times those that aren't organized have a hard time completing tasks or even staying focused. There will always be a distraction of some sort that will not allow you to function at your highest capacity, whether you try to do too many things at once or not prioritizing your tasks. It all boils down to your thought and mental organization. To combat this shortcoming, I'd recommend that you start by writing down and prioritizing your goals and tasks. Doing this will give you direction. I want you to stop for a moment and write down your goals and review them at least three times a day. The next thing would be to eliminate your obvious distractions such as phones, tv, radio, and even other people that are bothering you. This will open your mental space and allow you to focus on the task at hand. This part of the process is usually the toughest; our minds are conditioned to whatever we do most frequently. You have to fight it and put 100% of your focus on the task at hand. After doing this time and time again, you will become submerged in your work. You will have formed a habit, a habit that will have a significant effect on your productivity. By this time, other things in your life will transform as well; your mood will be better, your time will feel like it was well spent on everything you choose to dedicate your time to. It will be like a brain cleansing like you just dumped all of the garbage from your brain and replaced it with something more healthy and meaningful.

Time Is Money

You can always make up for any money you lost, but you can never buy back wasted time. Don't spend too much time on the small things, and don't waste your time on low-paying tasks. Please don't get this confused with you being too superior for any task. Low-paying tasks are those you can outsource; because of the amount of time it'll take you to do it, you could hire someone for it, pay their rate, and make more money doing more lucrative tasks. If you can make $500 an hour, you should never take an hour out to cut your grass. Pay someone $40 or so to do the task for you; while it will drop your profit margins, you are still coming out on top. This is a part of the "work smart, not hard" concept. Once your hourly rate increases, outsource more and more and watch your hourly rate consistently increase. You are now in control of your time and maximizing your value. Don't get caught up in the numbers; I want you to understand the concept of what I am saying.

How much is an hour worth to you right now? How can you increase it? If you said by multiplying your time, you are correct. Many people have never heard of the concept of multiplying their time. The concept of multiplying your time is elementary math. Let's say that you work 40 hours a week as an individual. Now, what if you had three more people on your team also working 40 hours a week. Now that brings you to four people working 40 hours a week which equals 160 hours. On average, you'll generate 100 dollars an hour for the business. On an average week by yourself, you will make $4,000 give or take. Now with a team of 4 and everybody doing roughly the same amount of productivity, you can bring in $16,000 a week. Deduct your expenses and payroll, and I'm pretty sure you're still making a nice profit to reinvest in your business and repeat this process. I am using these arbitrary numbers as an example to paint a clear picture. Feel free to plug in numbers to reflect your reality. We were never taught to work smart, just hard. There is a better way, people. Become the master of your money, not a slave to it. Put systems in place that can work and make you money when you are not around. The key is to find freedom, and the best way to do so is to have some predictable and repeatable process.

Circle Of Influence

We are heavily influenced by the people with which we spend the most time. If you are hanging around a group of goal-oriented individuals, it will rub off on you. Or if you are with people who are not managing their time properly, you will eventually squander your time. Either way, it rubs off on you sooner or later. We are quick to gravitate towards people with similar energy or value systems. If you allow people who have bad or time-wasting habits to enter into your personal space long enough, you will notice the difference. It is not something that will go unnoticed. If you strive to be a top performer and be the best version of yourself, you should be aware of the people you spend most of your time with.

When I was younger, I'd spend time with people that were closest to me. In my neighborhood, there were many bad influences and habits for you to choose from. So it was just a matter of time before you eventually chose one and lived with it. As a teen, I loved playing basketball, so all of my friends were into basketball as well. We'd get up early and play basketball wherever we could until the street lights came on. As we grew older, everyone went their separate ways, and most chose a path that would eventually land them in jail or a graveyard. As I saw the change happening, I found myself with a different group of people. This cycle continued as I grew, and my interest changed. Everyone will go down their path during their growth process. Some people will keep some of the same friends, and others will have a completely different circle in the next 1-3 years. You should seek to meet new people, and not just be around the same people your whole life. Don't get this confused; I'm not saying leave your current circle. Just look outside of your circle for other opportunities to grow if the growth isn't happening within your circle.

You can have many associates from multiple walks of life. Learning to speak different languages is key to survival and your growth. When I say other languages, I'm talking about various subjects and expertise. Having a diverse group of associates and friends is a great way to achieve this lifelong advantage. I am a master at doing this; if I am around individuals speaking on things that I am unfamiliar with, I instantly become a sponge. I take mental notes and research things I'm unfamiliar with. Once you begin researching one thing, it can easily lead to many other things that will expand your knowledge. If you are putting yourself around the right people, then it's only a matter of time before you pick up some useful information. Choose your immediate circle wisely; don't go for convenience or familiarity. Don't box yourself in because of fear of what you don't understand. Allow yourself to learn from others and become active in new circles of individuals with the same interests but from different walks of life. Building your network is one of the best things you can do in life. It requires no capital, and it will help you build a new set of skills and knowledge.

Be Intentional

To live a fulfilling life, you must be intentional in the actions you take. You are the person that will make the decisions that will either work for you or choose ones that will work against your anticipated future. We're faced with many circumstances daily. They come in the simplest forms, such as deciding whether we'll eat out or cook or whether we'll work out or see a movie. The decision you make is all dependent on what's most important to you at that time. There may be habits that we'd like to break, but choose not to and use excuses as to why we haven't changed. If you want something bad enough, you will make the shift, no matter how difficult it may be. Once you make that shift and continuously do so, you are now intentional in your growth. Our thoughts become our actions, and our actions will eventually become our habits, and our habits our reality, but remember consistency is the key. Doing something once or twice doesn't help; we will go right back to our old way of doing things. Think about the things that you do now. They are build-ups of years of implementation.

Make the right decisions that will produce the results you want for yourself, not just right now but in the future. Have you ever made a tough decision before? One that was hard to make, it may have taken days, weeks, or even months to build up the courage to finally pull the trigger. No matter how tough it may have been, you knew it was the right decision and would benefit you in the long run. Whatever that moment was for you, that was a time of you being intentional; you made the best decision for yourself and your future. You identified something that you wanted to change in your life, and you decided to make that change. There will always be resistance when you disrupt your regular schedule, but that disruption is required for your growth. Once you are intentional in one area, it will affect other areas of your life. What if I told you that you could have everything that you've been struggling to get by being intentional in your actions from this day on? Would you believe me and make that change? Well, surprise!!!! Everything you've been struggling to accomplish will happen once you become intentional in your actions. Strategically plan your next move so that you can get closer to that one thing you've been craving. Make sure that your intentions are in alignment with your vision of the optimal you.

GO GET IT

"I gotta grind, won't stop. Hustle won't quit. Shine like no other I be on some otha s***."(TI, Go Get It)

This is a favorite song of mine and the motto that I live by, GO GET IT and NEVER QUIT! Go out there, hustle and grind to achieve an audacious goal by any means. Don't stop until you reach that goal. There is no such thing as quitting in my dictionary. If I know that you're a quitter, I will cut you out of my inner circle with no hesitation. I don't need that energy around me. I need go-getters, hustlers, people taking constant strides to reach something bigger and better. I don't care if you're crawling towards something, DON'T STOP; keep your body moving. Never get content with a comfortable lifestyle. Once you are comfortable, get uncomfortable again, that's how you will continuously grow. It's like working out; you gradually add weights once the others get too easy, treat your life the same way. There are no easy paths in this thing called life. It is much easier to take the path with the least resistance and just hit cruise control through life. The easy path usually leads to a scene that is nothing above average. If you want exceptional results, you must do what the average won't do. You have to be willing to be different, don't go out to that party, put in the extra hours. Like the late great Nipsey Hussle said, "Dedication, hard work, plus patience." I don't think that would ever change if you want to achieve anything beyond average; there is no magic wand that you can wave to make your dreams a reality. The magic wand is you getting up off your ass, stop making excuses, and getting in the field to do the work yourself. If you want something done to your standards, you have to do it yourself.

As humans, we are naturally scared of things that seem difficult, but once that difficulty approaches, there are two types of people: those that tackle the challenges and learn then, then those that run away from challenges and fold. When you choose to turn your back on a challenge and go the other way, you are just delaying the process. You will still have to go through the same obstacles whether you wait or not if you are putting something off because you are scared of doing the work or don't know what to do. Know that you will face the same learning curves and challenges once you proceed on your journey, so you are better off starting the moment it becomes a thought. The time you are wasting can be the time you are growing and moving closer to who you want to become. You can read all of the books, watch all of the videos, and receive advice from the best of the best, but it all means nothing if you fail to take action. Do you know how many people have a lot more knowledge than those who have done great things? Let me tell you that more people have studied and learned everything they need to be successful. The only thing they lack is the drive to take action and make it happen. Hard work beats talent every time, so if you are getting up and doing the work every day, it will pay off in the future.

I am a firm believer in never giving up and everyone achieving their happiness. Whether that happiness comes from operating a successful business or having the freedom of doing whatever you want on your terms. There will always be people around you telling you what you can or can't do, and why you shouldn't waste your time. First, I'd say you cut them out of your life because you don't need that energy as you commence this journey. Second I'd say use it as fuel to prove them wrong. Show all your doubters and haters that you can achieve all that they said you wouldn't, and much more. When I say get it, GO OUT THERE AND GET IT! Not that half-ass when you feel like it. I'm talking about going broke for what you believe in, sacrificing, and the delay of gratification for you to reach that bigger goal. You're willing to drown for a brief period to eventually build that ship that's going to take you across the globe. That's my meaning of "Go Get It". That same mentality that both Kobe and Jordan showed on the basketball court is what I'm talking about. I'm speaking of the fact that I will not lose and will do anything necessary to win. You must understand that it's all out here for us to take it, so ask yourself, "What am I waiting for?" You said that you'd do it later months ago, I won't allow you to give up on yourself that easy, put this book down and take that first action step. You owe it to your future self. You know, the one you keep fantasizing about, you see yourself as this individual all the time, but you aren't doing what you need to do to get there. No more excuses, only results.

How To Get It

If you've never been the ambitious, self-starter type, it may be a bit difficult in the beginning to develop that go-getter mentality, and it takes time. You must make a plan, have a clear vision, and build a great foundation from the beginning. Whenever I set a new goal or take on a new challenge, I treat it like building a house. I design my blueprint, make sure my base is solid and build on top of that. I make sure that I have the right education on the subject, the right team of people, etc. Ensuring that you build a solid foundation is sometimes hard when you don't have the knowledge or resources required to take on such a task. Yes, you'll learn on the job, but you'll make mistakes that you could have prevented if you had more knowledge on the subject. I am speaking from pure experience. I started a business with zero knowledge and made almost every mistake I could. I knew nothing about paying taxes and owed the BOE(Board Of Equalization) $4800. I knew nothing about budgeting, my first company consistently ran out of money, and sometimes I would use my personal finances to fund it. I thought marketing was just about posting on social media, and that's it. Despite all of these mistakes, I never quit; I kept going after it and learned along the way. Eventually, I had to step back and restructure things. I put systems in place, made everything streamline, and had some type of system in place that made sense.

With your plan in place, you must now back that plan with action steps to help you inch closer to the big goal. Many times we confuse these steps for monstrous steps. That couldn't be further from the truth. Sometimes, the steps required at some parts of your journey are what you work on but are invisible to others - the long nights of educating yourself, researching, and reviewing the decisions you've made. These are all parts of the process and can't be skipped or overlooked. If you skip over them, you will find yourself doubling back to implement them into your overall plan. That's why I wrote this book, to aid you so that you don't have to make those small mistakes. Of course, you will make mistakes, but the mistakes will be less costly than they would have been.

Consistency and persistence will get you to where you want to be and allow you to get the things you desire. Repeatedly hammering at a tree is a sure way to knock it down, whether quickly or slowly. Remaining humble and keeping that same work ethic once you've achieved it determines how long you'll stay on top and build a loyal fan base. We love heroes who act as if they're average; it makes us feel like we can touch and connect with them. While we admire those of a larger caliber, we feel like we can't reach them, so it is more like a fantasy than a reality. Don't even mention being their equal. It is a beautiful feeling when you can call your idols your rivals. You climb yourself up the ranks and are now peers with those that you looked up to. It's a beautiful feeling, but that feeling won't come to you. You have to go towards it.

How Ambitious Are You?

Are you the play it safe type? You know, the type of person that likes a predictable outcome, something secure and consistent. Or do you like to bet the whole hand on the first roll and worry about the rest later? You know that the reward is bigger than the risk. Whichever category you belong to, there is no right or wrong; each one has negatives and positives. Like any split decision, there will be pros and cons to the decisions we make in life. The basis of us making these decisions has a lot to do with our personality types. Our personalities come from our experiences and upbringing. Though it differs from one person to the next, the cautious types were usually raised in a strict household where their parents didn't take any nonsense and established early that they were the boss. While the more free-willed type was raised in a home where they could explore, and the parents gave them a little more lead way on their leash. I won't get too deep on the subject; I'd like to get back to the point of your ambition. When you were a teen, were you always playing it safe, or were you out exploring things and trying new things and seeing what worked for you? Of course, there are still exceptions to every rule, but these principles apply to most people in a group.

You must get out of your shell if you are the 'play it safe type,' try something new, and don't be scared of what others may say or think. I can relate because I was once this individual, shy and quiet; I didn't speak up most of the time. I eventually grew out of it, and I noticed that it had a lot to do with a lack of confidence. I always had a preconceived notion of what others were thinking or would think of me in my mind. I slowly outgrew this thinking by just doing, doing what I wanted, and not worrying about others' opinions. In doing so, I gained more respect and self-confidence. This was one of the most pivotal moments in my life. As it allowed me to become the new version of myself that I always wanted to be, which I never thought I could be. Taking small steps such as speaking out within groups with which you are comfortable. These people are your friends, family, and anyone with whom you can let your guard down. These individuals will be shocked but will respect you at the same time. Besides, you deserve to be respected; you are always the observer and have a point of view that others don't realize. We are re-adjusting your habits; you are used to playing it safe and laying low. While you can still lay low, let your presence and opinion be known. While you'll always be the quiet one, others around you will know that you mean business when you speak up. This will translate into the rest of your life and open up many doors that were locked before. Your confidence will grow as you become more comfortable with this newfound power that you possess. The things you were petrified to pursue will no longer be boulders to you but peanuts. If this describes you, take these steps and turn your life around and feel the breath of fresh air that goes into your lungs.

Now all of my outgoing, life of the party individuals, I have this advice for you. In a social setting, that is fine, but you must learn to tone it down in certain circumstances. It's ok to let your presence be known, but at the right time. This kind of energy can push some people off. You've been this way your whole life, so it is hard for you to flip the card. You must become a chameleon and blend with your environment, knowing the right and wrong times to open up. There are strengths and weaknesses with every personality type, and your strength is drawing attention, but make sure it's the proper attention. Once you master this, you will be unstoppable. Listening is an art; it requires a lot of discipline and patience. Practice it on a small scale; try it with your spouse or a family member. Just become a sounding board for them, don't interrupt them, and watch your relationships grow stronger. Now you appear to care about their problems genuinely. It's a tactic I use all of the time; I'll listen to individuals, mirror what they said with what they just asked me, and say a little something here and there. By doing this, they think that I am an angel. Whether you are listening or not, they will never know because you just repeated what they told you and made them talk even more. This will work wonders for you in life; it will create a balance that wasn't there before that you can now use to your advantage.

Don't Play It Safe

I don't believe in playing it safe, and I don't believe in 'what if it doesn't work'? To me, that's just planning to fail. I go into situations looking at the finish line, figuring how I'm going to reach it. I'm not looking down at the sharks and alligators that are there ready to eat me once I fall because I don't plan on falling in the first place, but if I do, I'm winning that fight. I plan on reaching that goal line by any means necessary. The people that have gone ahead of me did it, I can do it too, and I'll be doing it my way, putting my touch on it. People that try to play it safe only get halfway across the playing field. You must give it your all and if that isn't enough, push even harder. Eventually, the extra skill required will appear; it's been deep inside you all along. The only way to activate it is by pushing yourself to new limits and going after what seems impossible. The universe always finds a way to pave a path for you. You must walk with confidence and know that you are entitled to all that you can imagine; you are owed these things. Despite what you were dealt, you will come out with the winning hand.

If you are cautious or careful, you will remain in your current situation. If you are happy there, be my guest, but if you are like me and want to get the most out of life, I'd say go after that dream at all costs. To get the most out of life, we must risk so much. Large risk equals big rewards. No risk, no reward. There is no right or wrong decision, but think about what you have to gain and lose by going for abundance, choose wisely. Not everybody is cut out for it. Some people can't handle the uncertainty; many people like the guarantee. That's fine, but if you are that person, let me ask you this, what are you being guaranteed? You may get a guaranteed paycheck, but what happens if the company goes bankrupt or you get sick, and your savings gets drained, or what if you don't have any savings? We form a plan, but we never plan for the unexpected. I say that I'd prefer to take control of my future and create wealth for myself instead of relying on a job that is no real security, in my opinion. The best security is the one that you curate for yourself.

Persistence

Would you stop your car while you are in the middle of traffic? I highly doubt it. Whether you are going slower, faster, or just keeping up with traffic flow, stopping isn't the first thought that comes to mind. Even if you get a flat tire or run into a detour, you continue to go in the direction of your destination. This is no different than when you are looking to achieve a goal in life. Will you stop just because something isn't going as planned, or it gets a little difficult? I'd hope not. The difficult circumstances that we are faced with from time to time are to test us on our true desire and passion for our intended goal. Tests are given to us in so many disguises, that we don't realize they are happening. These may come in forms such as financial hardship, uncertainty, heartbreak, or plain confusion, to name a few. Often, if we are depressed, sad, or not feeling accomplished, that is when we need to push harder at our goals. If you struggle with getting over a difficult time, dig deep and look for inner courage and pull it out. If you can identify this, then you've already won half the battle. Identify your purpose, something that you truly want, and back it with a plan to reach it.

Many people give up at the first sign of defeat or the moment they receive criticism from those close to them. You need to understand that not everyone will know what you are doing until it is done. There are very few people who will believe in your vision at its inception. The majority of people will see the work in progress and give you their opinion based on that and not on what you are building. So if you find yourself thinking about quitting, don't be so quick to find a new path; if you do, you will discover that the new direction has its different set of obstacles. If you genuinely believe in yourself and your plan, then continuing on your path no matter what is thrown in front of you is a no-brainer. For some, when they see things are getting a little difficult, they are quick to choose a different route.

A great example of this is someone who goes from business to business in hopes of getting rich quickly. Don't get me wrong; you may get lucky doing this. I can assure you that the lucky break is nothing compared to one gotten through persistence. If you choose to persist, you will eventually win every battle that you face. If not, most certainly, you'll be walking away with an L every time, and there will be no way around it. If you are a true believer in your abilities, persistence will come to you with no effort. If you have that fire and willpower within you to keep going no matter how rough the road may become, it is only a matter of time before you reach the zenith that you've always aspired to. All of the blood, sweat, and tears will all mean nothing once the goal has been met. If anything, it will give you the confidence to overcome any other challenge that may come your way. I want you to understand that you will get knocked down a couple of times in life, but all that matters is that you get up stronger and charge even harder. Eventually, you'll beat the opposition and prevail. No matter how hard the task may seem at the beginning or how unprepared you may feel, you can't lose if you never quit. Defeat is temporary; look at the many great athletes who may have been defeated the year before, just to come back the following year with even more force. This is a prime example of being persistent in your efforts to reach your goal despite criticism or being defeated. Give it all that you've got and if you fall, get back up, shake yourself off and go harder. You owe it to yourself to not give up, so if that road seems a little rough, don't choose a new destination. Just switch the route and reach your goal.

IDENTIFY YOU

Who are you? What defines you as an individual? Can you be bought, or you have morals and standards that you stand for? Whatever works for you, just own up to it. Some people just want money, others want fame, some want freedom, and others just want comfort and security. They chose these things because they feel that they will impact their lives in a way they'd like. There is no right or wrong answer to this. There are no two humans on earth that are identical in their way of thinking. Don't be afraid to be who you are. The moment you own up to the real you, the more free and comfortable you will be. Have you ever been in an uncomfortable situation where you just weren't yourself or felt like if you were not true to yourself, things would come off wrong? I learned that there is a way to be you while also adapting to your current environment. You must act like a body of water; remain who you are, but adjust to your surroundings. I feel comfortable in a business meeting and the middle of the ghetto; I know how to adapt to my environment and survive. This trait requires you to educate yourself to become comfortable speaking on multiple topics and understanding people with different backgrounds. You don't need to be an expert; just have a little understanding. This way, you'll know which crowds you'll be comfortable around when to be quiet and listen, and this will also improve you personally, not just professionally. You will always be in a circle where you are knowledgeable, but not the smartest and will be able to soak up as much information as possible. I used to be afraid of not being the smartest in a group until I noticed that I became much smarter by not being the smartest one in the mix. Soon this became a habit and happened naturally. I purposely seek out circles filled with those who are ahead of me on their journey or those who have lived through things and have a great philosophy of life. I will look for these groups and find a way to be a part of them. It doesn't have to be a lifelong friendship; it is just enough that my face is now familiar.

Learning from others who are ahead of you or have the same thinking pattern is key to continuous growth. Even when you are on the same level as someone, you can still learn from their experiences and perspective. This thinking will get you much further in life; you will learn the true benefit of not judging a book by its cover. I used to look at someone's appearance and judge them based on that alone, not realizing that this way of thinking was shallow. I discovered this when I began to get more into exotic and higher-end cars, going to car meet-ups and meeting people in that world; I noticed that they aren't always dressed in the latest fashion trends. Most of the time, they dressed very modestly or had no fashion sense at all. They weren't trying to be a trophy in the room. If I didn't know this, I would've never paired them with the cars that they owned. This helped me dramatically discover myself; I was no longer driven to believe that I needed the latest trends to appear to be of a higher caliber than I was. I learned to stay true to myself and be the best me. It doesn't matter how others may view me; if they are genuine people, they will not base their opinion on the material things that are in their face.

Soul Search

More and more people are becoming more concerned with their mental health. It has become a trend for people in recent years to soul search. We are getting more in tune with our spirits and mental well-being, but what does that mean? I've been soul searching a few times to re-learn myself. The moment I thought I knew myself, I grew and became a new person I was not familiar with. This comes with growth, which will continue to happen in life. Over the years, I've lost myself, was clueless and depressed many times. During one of my downhill slides, I dug deep within, and at that moment, I understood the purpose of soul searching. My awakening brought me to realize that I was searching for my true purpose in life this whole time. That thing that I am truly at peace with no matter where I am in life. What is something that I am passionate about? I thought it was music, fashion, and basketball during the earlier times of my life. While these were all things that I loved at one point, they weren't the thing I was truly searching for. I was searching for that thing that will bring me true joy. You know, that thing that will warm your soul and make you feel fulfilled no matter what. That one thing that you'd do willingly even if money weren't involved. You can love something and still feel empty, feeling like something bigger is missing. It was at this moment that I began to look at life differently. I wanted all of my actions from thereon to be purposeful. My inner part opened up; I became more compassionate, caring, and a better human overall. I slowly became a new person I was unfamiliar with but was starting to like and embrace.

If you aren't aware of soul searching, how can you do it? This question posed a challenge for me. It made me think hard and long, trying to find a way to put soul searching into actionable steps. One of the first things you must do is identify your current mental state, internal feelings, and the direction that you'd like to go. What is your peace or sanctuary? Do you have something that you feel at ease with and will do for free that brings you fulfillment? I'm talking about something with real meaning, whether you make a change for yourself or the world. For example, I am relaxed when I hear other people's life stories because it aligns with my mission of helping people. If you don't have one, that is the first step. Next, you must learn to control your inner thoughts and feelings, making you not allow minor things to disturb your peace. Once this step is mastered, you are well on your way to discovering the inner you. I want to emphasize this step because many daily factors can quickly make your day go south. Understanding that this is all controlled by your reaction to a situation will make this easier on yourself. I know this from experience; I used to have a horrible temper and would snap quickly. I began meditating and continuously told myself(even to this day) that I will not allow anything to steal my mental freedom and peace. I also got really in tune with myself and understood that the energy I put out would reflect what I receive. Next, you must find a positive in all situations. This can be the toughest part of the process. This part requires you to be the bigger person even if the other person is wrong. You will learn that it is not wise to argue with someone because people from the outside can't tell who's the fool. And fools will never believe that they are wrong, so they will argue with you for hours. Leaving it alone and channeling your energy towards the positive will bring more positive and beneficial experiences into your life. The quality of people you attract will change, the opportunities that come your way will be much richer. The inner you is your motor; it will keep you moving when you feel depleted or give you that energy when you feel that you have nothing left to give. Make sure you are taking care of it because it will take care of you.

Discover Your Purpose

We were all put on this earth for a reason, which is much bigger than ourselves. Whether you know it or not, you have a purpose in this game of life. I discovered my purpose 28 years into my life. It was brought to my attention that I was put on this earth to help others better themselves. Let me explain; I have often been called upon for my opinion or input on many situations and scenarios in other people's lives. People valued and trusted my opinion even if it wasn't my expertise; they just liked that I was well-versed on various topics and my ability to see things from a wide-angle as they often zoomed in on minor details. I sat back and thought to myself, "I truly enjoy listening to others and offering positive advice." I am fulfilled if I can help someone else achieve something greater or give them advice that will allow them the capability to move past a bump in the road. Not many people can say they have this gift and enjoy it. Most of the time, we are so busy with our problems that we don't have the mental capacity to sit and listen to someone else's problems and assist them in their situation. I am different, while like any other adult, I have my problems, but I tend to put my issues to the side momentarily and assist others if I can; that is the selfless part of me. I don't neglect myself; I just disconnect from my problems, then become present and engaged with whoever I am assisting. I've always wanted to make the world a better place; this is my way of doing so. It always means a lot to me when I see others achieve their goals, and it is even more rewarding when I am a part of that victory.

Many people ask me, "How do I discover my purpose?" I have a few answers to this question. Before I go into it, let me say that some people never discover their purpose, and there is nothing wrong with that. A large number of people live fulfilling lives and never know their purpose. Some may argue and say that it isn't possible. Think about someone who has been on the job for 30 years; they come in happy, have a family, and live a pretty good life. Take family trips, have a home that they purchased, basically living the "American Dream." There is nothing wrong with this individual; they are happy and content with their lifestyle and see no reason to seek further satisfaction. This is a perfect example of someone happy without discovering their purpose. I'm pretty sure we all know someone like this. From the outside, this person is fulfilled, which may be the case, but not everyone in this position has even thought about their purpose. You start a career, have a family, now their wellbeing is your purpose and number one priority. The aspirations and dreams you had before are out the window, and having security for your family is most important.

You may say, "I want that, and I want to live a purposeful life." You must first realize that a purposeful life is an unselfish, people-serving, disciplined lifestyle. If you look for ways to better the world around you, not just your inner growth, more than likely, you are a selfless human being. This takes a tremendous level of maturity and growth. To care about how other humans are doing or how you can help make their life better is an act of selflessness. If you are in this mental space, great. If not, no worries. You must dig deep and find out if this is something that you truly want and bring the joy you are seeking. Don't let it be something you fake just to appear that you are living a purposeful life. If you genuinely want to be a servant to the people, then great. You are about to learn how you can do so.

Do you want to help people? If so, this section is for you. This journey of helping others is a challenge. You must first understand that you can't please everybody and that people are unpredictable. Have you ever had the best idea in your mind, then you presented it, and it was shut down? That will happen to you time and time again. You'll spend countless hours on something you are proud of, and it doesn't receive the response you anticipated. This can be discouraging, and many people quit after this happens repeatedly, thinking they don't have what it takes. You must develop a thick layer of skin and know how to look over these so-called failed attempts, go back to the drawing board and go right back at them again and again and again. Most of the time, it is the persistence and consistency that will get you over that hump. Do you honestly believe in your vision? Are you willing to hold on to everything because you are confident it will eventually emerge? If so, you should never let the thought of quitting fully develop in your brain. Once you do, you are opening a crack for more negative self-limiting beliefs to creep in. Keeping yourself motivated in the darkest times is key to overcoming the treacherous journey you are embarking on – a journey that will leave you with an endless amount of joy if you stick to it. The money, cars, clothes, and other material things are nice, but there is a different feeling of joy when someone tells you that they didn't give up because of you. After receiving this type of praise, you will be looking for more ways to help more people transform their lives.

The Disadvantage of Being Average

Some of us are scared of being great because those around us are afraid to be great. We allow those around us to determine our altitude. We don't want to make others uncomfortable and fear the criticism we will receive because we are different. When you settle for average, you are saying that you just want to get to the level where you find comfort and become content. Like I've said many times before, THERE IS NOTHING WRONG WITH THAT! If that is where your happiness resides, great! If you are just settling for average because others around you are average, you are doing yourself a disservice - you are hindering your growth. Many people don't achieve their full potential because they are afraid of standing out; they want to fit in with their friends. Or maybe even fear what people would say about them for desiring heights that usually aren't meant for the average person to reach.

Don't be afraid of being amazing; let your greatness be on the highest display for the world to see. You will inspire other people in ways that you can't imagine. When I began speaking, I was scared. I was afraid of how I'd sound, what others would say, and how people would perceive me. This fear went out the window once I began. The moment I decided just to start doing instead of creating problems that didn't exist, is the moment that I felt free and felt like I could do even greater things. With this courage came confidence; this confidence allowed me to have bigger dreams than I had previously had. Others started reaching out, saying that I was an inspiration to them; they had decided to let go of fear and reach their fullest potential as well. If I had decided to remain average, none of these things would be possible. You wouldn't be reading this book today if I had decided that I would settle for average when I knew that I had dreams of being more outstanding.

I still deal with fear today, but the difference is how I respond to fear. Instead of tucking my tail in, I take a deep breath and face it head-on. I look fear right in the eye and remind myself that my fear of remaining in the same place is much greater than fighting to get to my next level. I'd prefer to come out with a few bruises from battling for what I want than remain unscathed in the same place. I have now built up the strength that I need to take on even greater challenges. Facing my fears allows me to consistently build the strength I need to compete with obstacles I'm yet to encounter. The moment you choose to move from average, you begin to become the individual you need to be in order to elevate to the next level. The universe is usually working two times as hard as you are to meet you halfway. So when you feel like you aren't getting anywhere, just look back at where you started and be proud that you aren't there anymore. You are in a progressive motion, and every little step counts. These small stops can accumulate into big steps. No one ever takes huge strides; those huge strides are a combination of all of the small steps taken in the background. Understanding this gives you a mental break that is much needed. We need to get out of our heads, believe in our vision and our abilities to overcome anything life throws at us.

THE BRAND OF YOU

D id you know that you are a brand? Do you look at yourself as such? It doesn't matter if you are selling a product, service, or yourself you must first understand that you are a brand! If you aren't recognized, people won't purchase from you. In today's market, people buy from the individual, not a logo (unless you are established). I learned this the hard way when I was running my clothing brand. I did well during the days of Twitter. I was selling like crazy; I couldn't keep up with the demand. Eventually, Twitter started to fade away as Instagram came in and became the go-to social media platform. Being stubborn, I kept using the same practices. It continued to sell, but not as much. More brands were beginning to pop up, and now the market was getting saturated with competition. I didn't pay attention and kept using the same practices as I did with Twitter. I paid big time for this mistake. My business became a slowly sinking boat, and I was in the back scooping up water, tossing it over my shoulder just for it to roll right back to my feet. This was devastating for me; how could something I've poured my heart and soul into fail so miserably? I eventually came to the reality and decided to put the brand on hold.

When I put the business on hold, I had already begun speaking. I was now putting my message out there with my face and name. People became fans of me, so now all I had to do was build these relationships up slowly while providing content that they could benefit from. You don't have to be a celebrity to sell yourself, you may not know it, but you are always selling yourself somehow. You are trying to persuade someone to see something the way you see it, give you something, buy something from you. You are selling yourself in these situations. Have you ever gone back somewhere and was hoping to be attended to by the same person every time you return? That person sold himself/herself to you. The more people you sell yourself to, the more your brand grows. Now you provide them with quality products, information, or services that they can use. They will share with the world, and your brand continues to grow. How strong is your brand with your target audience? How do you plan on growing this brand? These are a couple of questions you should be able to answer.

Building a brand is hard work; building your brand is more challenging and takes a lot of courage and confidence. First, you must get out of your head. You can talk yourself out of it before you even begin. I had my doubts and insecurities when I first started, but I had to beat my thoughts to overcome these distractions. Then I used the SWOT Analysis(Strengths, Weaknesses, Opportunities, Threats) to identify my best move to have the biggest impact. I tried many things that didn't work, but I believed in my capability to market myself so much that I kept going. Once you commit to increasing your brand's value, everything else usually falls in place at the right time along the process.

Your Reputation

What others think of you means so much when you are building your brand. Your reputation is what people say about you when you're not around; whether they'll tell others good things or bad things about you, word of mouth is the best promotion. Enough bad reviews about you or your business can diminish your reputation. It is tough to please everybody, so that should never be your intention. To uphold your name, you should develop a reputation of being true to yourself. The moment we steer away and do what we think others want, we lose ourselves. We are no longer true to our core values. Doing this kicks you out of your comfort zone. Have you ever done something just to please someone else and felt uncomfortable? This is the same feeling that will eventually arise once you opt for people-pleasing. When you stay true to who you are, you will build a little slower, but at the same time, you are building a solid fan base, people who like you for you and not a facade that they bought into.

So how do you build a good reputation? Simple, over-deliver what you tell people you will deliver. It doesn't matter if you promised a great product or service; consumers always love to get more than they were promised they would receive initially. In doing so, you will be creating a tribe of loyal customers and supporters. They will feel like they got more than what they paid for. As humans, we like to feel like we are appreciated and recognized. We don't want to feel like we are just a number or another dollar. There is true value in making people feel good. If you understand and practice that, you are well on your way to a positive and strong personal brand.

Selling Yourself

There was a time when people had this thing about the Illuminati; they felt that anybody who had managed to reach a great achievement level must've sold their soul to this group. This went on for years and may still have true believers today. This was their way of rationalizing how someone who breathes the same air has the same 24 hours as they do could attain such a great height in life. As if there was some chosen group that selected these individuals to become successful. While I genuinely believe that some things can be achieved very quickly if you know the right people, I also believe that you must sell yourself to people. You can have the most connected people in your corner, but if they don't believe in you, it wouldn't matter. Every day in life, we are selling ourselves, and we don't even know it. Every brand that you like has been sold to you. They've sold you a vision, emotion, or idea of something that they offer. I never understood this concept until I got into my mid 20's. I always thought that if you put something out, it looks good, people like it, and buy it. I failed to implement the most important step, selling. The moment I realized it, I took a different approach and gave people the human connection, and I connected with their pain points. I let them know that I was like them and that I had overcome things they are currently faced with and could teach them how to do it. I continued to show that I am an ordinary human being, showing them how I took an extraordinary approach. Showing that I was average made me relatable. I didn't come from a wealthy family; I am from a background of lack of education. I learnt real tactics that helped me excel in adulthood alongside gangsters and drug dealers though I managed to avoid their lifestyles. This normality made me human. Now I had to sell people on why I am worth buying from, what will I give you that will help you in your life today. The marketplace is crowded; people have thousands, if not millions, of options to buy the same thing you are selling; why buy from you? There comes the challenge, what distinguishing factors do you have that sets you aside from competitors? Your answers to these questions will be your selling point. This doesn't just apply to business; it applies to everything in your life. Whether that be a job, relationship or anything else you are trying to win.

Now think back on some interactions you may have had with people. Did they do a good job of selling themselves to you? Maybe your spouse sold you their point of view, or your child sold you on something they wanted. Whatever it is, think back on the times you've been sold to and the times when people failed to sell you on something. What made the difference between buying in and not buying in on it? Some of us are naturally better at selling while others have to put in a little extra work, know where you stand. The more familiar you are with something, see the value in it or see it solving a problem for you, the more you are inclined to buy. Apply these same rules to yourself. Do others see you as someone who can solve a problem or bring value to their lives? It is your job to position yourself to execute the sale. If you can sell, then you will never need money, remember that.

SEPARATING FROM THE PACK

To stand out, you must do what the average person isn't willing to do. If you don't know what that is, look at the people around you. If you are satisfied with the average results of your circle, mimic their actions, but put your twist on it. If you aren't happy and want more, do the opposite of what everyone else is doing, don't be afraid to go against the tide. They may talk about you behind your back or maybe even to your face, but don't let that discourage you. Stay true to your beliefs and blaze your path, and they will have no choice but to respect what you are doing. I am speaking from experience; when I decided to follow my passion of helping others, I was nervous. I worried about how people would look at me, what they'd say, and if they'll still respect me. I was taking on something unheard of for anyone from my neighborhood. I decided to do it, mute the outside noise, and follow my heart. First, they laughed, called me weird, a sellout, and called me an oreo (look up in the urban definition). It bothered me initially; I was hoping that they would catch on and understand what I was talking about. Until this day, most have not, and they are still in the same spot that they've been in for many years. Ultimately, I knew who I was on the inside and where I am coming from. I decided to become something other than what everyone else was, which is a product of my environment. I will always have my street tendencies and knowledge, but I am much more than that. The majority of my support comes from people I have never met me in person, and I am completely fine with it. I have helped far more people than I could even imagine; it is a true blessing to have people who have never met me appreciate the work I do. It is a humbling experience to see where I am coming from, where I am, and to see how bright my future looks from this point on.

If I can do it, so can you. You can't be scared of being different; just go for it. Here's the catch, you can't go halfway; go in with intentions of being the best at whatever you decide to do. Always compete with the person in the mirror, always raise the bar for yourself and never settle for less. I'm not saying that it will be easy, it will be challenging, and life will gladly kick your ass on multiple occasions. I do have great news, though; life will get tired of you coming back time and time again and will eventually give up. That is the moment where your opportunity meets preparation. It's up to you if you will take advantage of it or not; the window of opportunity doesn't stay open for too long. Those who were able to Separate From The Pack never lost their enthusiasm when they hit the floor. There is no secret to it; the secret is never to quit. Despite all obstacles, tragedies, or defeats you may face, keep striving for more. Never remain idle; make that engine work. If you never decide to control your life and move, life will take control over you. Life has taken control of the majority of the world's population. There is an abundance of people living below their potential. There is a graveyard full of dead dreams; make sure yours don't end up there.

Final Thoughts

Now that I've laid out the steps for you, what's next? Will you remain within the pack and ponder on your next move, or will you charge after whatever it is that you desire and pull away? The choice is yours, and it always has been. You have always had all of the power to pursue and conquer anything you can imagine and overcome any adversity you are faced with. Your confidence should be built up by now, and you should be in a different headspace to where you feel unstoppable. It may take a little longer to get there for some but continue to apply the practical steps laid out throughout this book, and you'll be fine. Make it a point to form new habits and do things a little bit differently than before. Write down all of your goals, pair them with actionable steps, persist, and they will manifest. Remember that patience and discipline is key; anything good doesn't come when you want it to. The great things will always hit you from the blindside. Those dark storms that are rough right now are all a test. You are being tested this very moment to see how bad you want it. It is much easier to stay in the same place and do what everyone else is doing. The real challenge is doing something that no one else dares to do. The moment you are comfortable standing out is when your real growth and separation begin to materialize.

I hope that what I covered in this book sparks that fuse in your mind for change and is enough information to give you a push away from being average. Change is always uncomfortable but good. The moment we make it out of that dark space, the sun will shine brighter than ever. Time spent in the dark is when your true character is built. We are presented with scenarios that may break most people. Only the strong will survive and come out better than before. A positive, abundance mindset will be essential for you to find that small crack of light. It will guide you and reconstruct your brain to one that you have always wanted. Above anything, BELIEVE IN YOURSELF. Believe in your process and journey; that belief will turn into a passion and drive. That passion and drive will guide you wherever your heart desires. How does that new you look? Looks good, right? Let your conscious mind and unconscious mind align with one another.

True success is bigger than us; it is bigger than the dreams we hold for ourselves. Yes, I've achieved some of my goals, but how many people did I help along the way? That is how I measure my success. How many people can say that my work has helped them? As I stated in Chapter 3, there is no right or wrong answer for your mission. Personally, I hope I achieved part of my personal goal with this book. I hope that at least one person has transformed their lives because of my efforts and contribution. I still listen to my own words now, so publishing this book does not make me perfect. I am human; I go through ups and downs as well. I don't have life figured out. I still need guidance and help with my problems. That is an even bigger inspiration to keep inspiring others because some of us may not have an outlet for our problems. Everyone doesn't have someone to call that'll give them the advice they need to hear. Many times I dealt with my problems all alone. No one even knew what was going on. At times I couldn't even describe what was going on because I didn't even know.

With this book coming to a close, it opens a new beginning for us all. How will your new chapter begin? Are you the author of your life and not bound to the barriers society has placed on you? Will the plot remain the same? Are the main characters changing? You are the author, so you decide the outline and make whatever revisions you feel are necessary. I've revised my life numerous times just to get to this point, which I'll probably revise again. Chapters have been moved, characters have been replaced, and plots have twisted. Miraculously, the story is still going, and here I am. Feeling better than before, but I have not reached my peak. I am continuously stuck between, I'm doing good, and I have to do more. I hope you aren't afraid to make some changes in your life, move things around and give yourself a fresh start. You were put on this earth to be all that you can be. We get one shot at this thing called life, one chance to get it right. Don't waste your chance. Right now, you may be part of a pack that you have outgrown or feel like you no longer belong within this pack. It is up to you and only you to take steps in the direction of separating from that pack. If stepping out and being a one-person pack is required of you to get to that next level, don't hesitate to do that. Those who go on to do the unthinkable had to decide about standing out from the crowd.

There will be people pulling you back, making you feel bad for wanting something different, and even people physically pulling you back in. It is your right to fight back and break away for the better of your future. Close your eyes(seriously close them) and create the grandest vision in your head of how your best life looks. What does it look like? Are you traveling the world, is your family happy and healthy, do you have financial security, how do you feel internally? You are the one that will bring yourself whatever you desire. The best life you can think of is waiting for you. That is what you deserve, now go out there and Separate From The Pack.

www.ingramcontent.com/pod-product-compliance
Lightning Source LLC
Chambersburg PA
CBHW021338090426
42742CB00008B/647